In Love with Life

The Vanderbilt Library
of American Philosophy

offers interpretive perspectives on the historical roots of
American philosophy and on present innovative developments in
American thought, including studies of values, naturalism, social
philosophy, cultural criticism, and applied ethics.

General Editor
Herman J. Saatkamp, Jr.

In Love
with Life

*Reflections on
the joy of living and why
we hate to die*

John Lachs

Vanderbilt University Press

NASHVILLE AND LONDON

First Edition 1998

98 99 00 01 02   5 4 3 2 1

Publication of this book was supported
by a gift from James P. Gray II

This publication is made from paper that meets the minimum requirements of ANSI/NISO Z39.48-1992 (R 1997)—Permanence of Paper
for Printed Library Materials. ∞

Library of Congress Cataloging-in-Publication Data

Lachs, John.
    In love with life : reflections on the joy of living and why we
hate to die / John Lachs. -- 1st ed.
    p. cm. -- (The Vanderbilt library of American philosophy)

  ISBN 0-8265-1328-X (alk. paper)
  1. Life. 2. Death. I. Title. II. Series.
  BD431 .L229 1998
  128--ddc21

                                    98-25379
                                    CIP

Published by Vanderbilt University Press
Printed in the United States of America

To my family, friends, and community,
for making life vibrant

Contents

Preface

While discussing some moral problems connected with ending life, a person once asked me why we so hate to die. Before I could think of a circumspect answer, I heard myself saying, "Because we are in love with life."

On later reflection, this idea of passionate devotion struck me as particularly helpful in trying to understand our complicated and intimate relation to existence. Much as we may complain about our condition or feel victimized by fortune and fellow humans, we simply love being alive. To love life is to love the activities of which it consists and to hope for more.

This book is as much an expression of that love as a chronicle of it. The energy that is life needs no justification: the rush of events and the swirl of our activities create an excitement that is its own reward. Yet there are times when energy lags and we face, if not a dark night, at least an endless, insipid, gray afternoon of the soul. At those times, reading the pages that follow may be of help.

When we are called to make momentous choices or to reconcile ourselves to sadness, loss, and death, thinking through the magnificence of our existence may refocus or even rekindle our vitality. Taking delight in small achievements and in the flowering of energy everywhere can help us face the darkness, which sometimes surrounds us, with courage and in peace. My reflections aim to be a celebration of life that, like a good party or contagious laughter, grabs hold of spectators and pulls them in. It will have done its job if it contributes a little to the joy of life or at least helps us cope with its pains.

Life is at the bottom of things . . . indestructibly powerful and joyous.

FRIEDRICH NIETZSCHE,
The Birth of Tragedy

1

Loving Life

Young Dogs

Young dogs, sniffing the air and tumbling at the entrance of a mall, quickly attract a crowd. Full of energy but uncoordinated, they crash into shoes, lick the hands that pet them, stumble off the curb. Dignified businessmen catch a glimpse of the delight and smile as they move on. Young girls stop to hug the balls of fur; salesclerks watch the squirming puppies and the girls. The dogs are so alive that their vibrancy transfixes everyone. Seeing such innocent, unreflective bliss blots out all worries and fills us with joy in life.

Up and down the street, throughout the city, everywhere in the world, people delight in their activities. They talk and swim, build houses and see the sunrise from them, make music and make love. They hug their children, argue about politics, and move to the beat that comes from passing cars with self-forgetful intensity. They plan and play and eat and work and even reminisce with fire in their souls. Their energy cannot be contained. Their spirit animates everything they think and touch. Humans live at white heat, aflame with life and love.

We love life in others and in ourselves; we are in love with life. Like good lovers, we embrace it with total devotion, committing all of our being to its service. We guard it jealously and caress it with a passion we cannot understand and hardly believe we can feel. When our love is reciprocated and life is good, we feel joyously fulfilled. We need nothing beyond such happiness. When life threatens to leave, we act like wounded lovers unable to see why our beloved should abandon us. Summoning all our energy, we acknowledge no rules and no morality in the fight to make sure that life remains.

Some think that we merely tolerate life or that we consent to it only grudgingly, in light of the alternative. Those who speak of a struggle for survival depict existence as a series of grim fights that prepare us only to fight again. The German philosopher Schopenhauer views eating as but a way to avoid death by starvation, and the British thinker Hobbes maintains that in its natural condition life is nasty and insecure.

Common human experience does not support such accounts. Children throw themselves into their activities with self-forgetful glee. Adults and even old people delight in doing whatever they can do well. The search for new thrills and challenges constitutes a significant theme in human history. The pain of living of which the great Greek thinker Aristotle speaks is typically restricted to the sick; for the most part, as Aristotle himself knew, pleasure accompanies what we do, so long as we do it voluntarily and well.

If we merely liked or tolerated life, we would be satisfied with however much or little we may get of it. But loving it means that we ceaselessly seek the activities of which it consists. This is the surest mark of love: lovers never get enough of their beloveds. They create new opportunities for togetherness, new activities to share. They feel satisfied in their union, but never sated. More of it, they think, is always better and an infinity would be just right.

Even those who complain a lot love much of what they do. The sick welcome improvement not only as a release from pain but also as a glorious sign that life is returning. When healing is far away, hope is enough to give us bursts of joy. And when even sensible hope has fled, kind words from the doctor suffice to cheer the soul. We do not just *like* to live, we are *in love* with life, in deep, passionate love. To be in love with life is to love being alive.

I offer no theories about whether this love is unique to humans, though, generally speaking, less is the special possession of our species than we like to think. When we watch young dogs at play, can we believe that they do not find life joyous? Yet when puppies turn into dogs, they are satisfied to sleep much of life away, while many humans stay up at night looking for challenges or meeting them. It is possible that the energy of life burns more brightly or for more hours a day in humans than in other animals. This is a mixed blessing, of course: being in love is exciting, but not without risk and pain.

Our love of life may be a madness, as perhaps all passions are. But for us it is, in the American philosopher

In Love with Life

George Santayana's words, a normal madness. By some reckonings, slow, sleeping animals may well be better off than humans. Equanimity is a great revenge on a world we can't control. The energy of humans makes them care intensely, and those who care give hostages to fortune. Yet letting things matter makes for an especially rich life: living at white heat has its compensations.

I also offer no theories about whether love of life is universal among humans. I do not wish to say that members of other cultures want to live less or that they live less passionately than we do. But I note that the intensity with which modern Westerners throw themselves into the activities of life and the wide range of these activities suggest that we enjoy (and suffer from) particularly powerful drives. Though perhaps people in all ages and in all societies have experienced passion, not all cultures have the concept of being in love, and certainly not all share our enthusiasm for the wonderful variety of life. I leave cross-cultural judgments of who is better off to those who think we are not doing well.

Loving What We Do

What does it mean to be in love with life? First and foremost, it is to love the activities of which life consists. Obviously, not everyone loves every activity. This is why the opportunity to choose and the wisdom of one's choices play such central roles in good lives. Yet everyone loves some activities and, given a chance, can learn to love more. Much of this love is spontaneous: eating, playing, touching each other, making happy noises, watching the dance of light, building things up and knocking them down delight us as soon as we start doing them, without the need for any training period.

Under normal circumstances, even infants enjoy their activities as soon as they are able to engage in them. They don't value them for their use: they like cooing and gurgling just as much as they love to eat. They draw no distinction between activities they start spontaneously and those that are responses to external circumstance. Everything seems to be done with total involvement: crying and laughter engage the entire body, bottle or breast call each part of the little being to attention and exertion. Even the smallest tickle evokes delighted grimaces, giggles, and the waving of arms.

Children at play may be the best example of self-forget-ful love of life. Worry is a sign of maturity, an expression of concern that nothing is as it seems. We learn to worry when we first suspect that we must look beyond the delight of the moment or that the good is about to be ambushed. Children are, of course, perfectly aware that nothing lasts for-ever; even the longest day of play ends when it's time for supper. But, fortunately for their peace of mind, children don't worry about the end when they are in the midst of things. Their happiness is sustained because it never occurs to them to focus on anything other than what they do at the moment.

Absorption in well-loved activity is what makes child-hood the best-loved season of many lives. Not having to do much one doesn't want is a great privilege, a luxury per-mitted only to lucky children and irresponsible adults. No careful observer can doubt that young people love life by loving their activities. Even when their days are filled with illness or misfortune, a moment's respite is enough to throw them into single-minded concentration on some beloved game. Adults who can imitate this childlike trait improve their lives to an astonishing degree.

We are born as squirming charges of energy seeking release. Education and social life direct our energies to suitable objects and objectives. The activities we learn are indefinitely various; left alone, most of us would never have thought of most of them. Would watching gauges in a boiler room or stitching the upholstery of cars have occurred to anyone as a good thing to do? Yet we find ourselves doing such things to make a living or to meet our obligations. Can we suppose that we love these activities and, through them, our lives?

We clearly do. Many of the activities social life teaches are easy to enjoy. It takes little to see the point of kissing and conversation, of driving cars and driving with a basketball down the court. But life becomes hard when much of it is filled with things we have to do to make ends meet. Going to work when we don't like what we have to do requires bitter discipline, perhaps the discipline of hunger as the alternative. Philosophers have long worried about the sadness this involves and the resulting waste of human lives. Karl Marx, who never did a stitch of such unwanted, fragmented work, denounced it as forced labor. The American philosopher John Dewey thought long and hard about what structural changes we would need to make in society to eliminate it.

The truth of the matter is that human psychology is constantly in the business of reducing misery. Perhaps out of self-defense, even the most obnoxious activities acquire a fringe of pleasure. At first, we may enjoy the satisfaction of a challenge met, and later, the predictability of a habit.

Loving Life

Even bad jobs afford companions-in-misery, to whom it becomes a pleasure to complain. The most devastatingly boring routines establish expectations of regular sequences that confer small satisfactions as they are met.

Society also hurries to our aid, heaping honor on all gainful employment. Most important perhaps, the delight of what we obtain with work, even if it is only money, spreads to the activity to make it bearable. A friend of mine who fights and haggles over trades for eight hours a day used to hate his job when he was young. He must have been good at what he did because he made a lot of money. He recently confessed that now he cannot wait to return from his vacation; he has come to see the insults and the haggling as delightful means to wealth.

We love life because we love the activities of which it consists. When the activities are indifferent or painful, we render them acceptable and even good. One great problem with retirement is that the activities at work we so love to hate define us and give us a hundred reasons to live. When they are removed, fishing is inadequate to take their place. Not surprisingly, many people die soon after retiring. Having little left to love, they have precious little to live for.

There is no reason to suppose, of course, that we love everything we must do. But we love much of it and certainly more than we let on. Our passivities bother us a great deal more than our activities: we like least not what we do but what happens to us. And there are terrible things that happen to people, some as a result of what others do. But even when misfortune strikes, working to overcome handicaps, ill fortune, fear, and disease leads us to activities we can love and enjoy.

7

In Love with Life

As traditional wisdom suggests, the problems of life can be converted into opportunities that lead us to do and experience what otherwise we could not even imagine. Without these problems, our minds would be simpler and we would have less to do, less to be proud of, and much less to love. To say this is not to justify the human condition, only to describe it.

Loving to Live Well

Loving life also means enjoying what life provides. The history of humankind is, among other things, the history of self-abnegation. Puritans want to have little to do with the pleasures of the body, and ascetics reject the allure of worldly goods. That they have to demonize otherwise desirable things is testimony to the unnaturalness and difficulty of what they try to do.

The body is the source of varied and largely innocent pleasures. Excess and careless perversion can, of course, subvert the happy life. But trying to make sure that we enjoy nothing physical is a task our nature frustrates at every turn. If we fast to assert control over the body, the first bite of food gives exaggerated joy. If we suppress the sexual urge by day, it finds an outlet in the middle of the night. The body overwhelms our resistance to its pleasures or tricks us into enjoying them in disguise.

The reason early moralists cautioned against enjoyment of physical pleasures is precisely because they are so powerful and alluring. Uncontrolled devotion to them does, indeed, interfere with social life and common responsibility. If we do not civilize these impulses, human existence can quickly descend to a level below that of animals.

Loving Life

The rule that we should relieve ourselves of liquid waste only in special places in the house and not in the kitchen or the dining room, for example, is not an arbitrary repression of urinary freedom but the sensible attempt to separate importantly different functions. In the name of living well with each other, we must learn what can be done with whom and how and when.

Many of the customs that in time grow into taboos are, when viewed from a distant and disinterested perspective, adjustable. Whether sexual relations should be confined to marriage and whether marriage should be restricted to heterosexual, single-partner unions are questions we can abstractly debate. But it is clear that we cannot allow sexuality to serve as the only, and hence unimpeded, value in human relations, and it is equally clear that we must devise some social structure for nurturing the young.

Changing established customs is often desirable or unavoidable. Technological, economic, and social circumstances constantly modify our ways and values; we feel their effect more keenly today than perhaps ever before. But total liberation from custom is either impossible or the road to madness. We must have some established ways of doing things, some edifice of values, some order in our lives. If the order that represses bodily pleasures leads to terrible consequences, we are justified in revising it. But we fool ourselves if we think that lifting every prohibition solves all of our problems.

One of the great drawbacks of despising the body is that it removes not only the worrisome excesses of physical life but also its rich rewards. This is a severe loss: it reduces the variety of what we can enjoy and diminishes the intensity of our love. The world is full of marvelous things that even puritans can appreciate. But the marvels of nature are not unconnected to the magnificence of the senses, by means of which we note and embrace them. The human body, when tied to the imagination, becomes a vibrant sense organ by which we participate in the beauty that surrounds us.

This mode of enjoyment is as different from cool objectivity as swimming in a moonlit pool differs from noting distant light shimmer on the waves. Those who don't love the body are at a distance from the world. Being uninvolved has its advantages, but the accompanying losses are devastating. Involvement means being interested in everything and delighting in every process and change.

The seventeenth century thinker Spinoza and some more recent writers feel overcome at how natural—how fascinating, how surprising, and yet how consistent with the course of nature—everything appears. This is one of the feelings that permit us to leave behind our concern for ourselves and for the narrowly local. It opens the past and especially the future as objects of our concern, as things to be interested in and to care about. People who identify their interests with the future of human life and with what is beautiful in the world live better and find it easier to die.

Loving and fostering the body provide another great advantage: those who do, double their pleasure. Everything we see or touch has an objective presence in the world, but also an immediate life in our senses. Objectively, airplanes are splendid devices of convenience and power. Kings of old would have offered their empires for an hour of what they enable us to do. But they are also silver birds and shimmering specks in the sky. Their vapor trails make them arrows that fly at thirty thousand feet. At a distance, they look like tiny toys; closer, they reveal intricate shapes and bulges that reflect the light. We can appreciate them both for what they do and for the splendid variety of their appearances.

The same is true of every other object. A plum bought at the store is also the ravishing taste of cold sweetness bursting in the mouth. A compact disk is also the sound of Mozart as it fills the soul. The waves of the sea are also a rhythmic rumbling and something dark that flowers into white.

Even obnoxious objects can, in this way, be converted into beauty: the annoying wall my window faces can suddenly resolve into an intriguing pattern of colors and lines. A few heroic thinkers even claim to have extracted the pure shape of pain from the body's complex reaction. They say that, focusing on it hard, they have been able to overcome or overlook their suffering. Natural childbirth may present a related phenomenon: it replaces the pain of wrenched muscles with more agreeable feelings of effort and control.

For reasons not easy to understand, many people sing the praises of antique virtues. They mean by these not the sort, such as courage and generosity, that Aristotle happily endorsed, but rather the austerity of making do without the advantages the modern world provides. It is better, they suppose, to take no medications, use no fertilizers, and buy no newfangled machines.

They view computers and fax machines not just as unnecessary luxuries but also as positive impediments to a simple and wholesome life. They prefer old telephones to new ones and bicycles to cars. They think that home-canned vegetables are better than what can be bought at the store and that if only we could rid ourselves of the unnatural offerings of new technology, we would enjoy better and more satisfying lives.

There is not a shred of historical evidence to support such beliefs. We all know that new technology brings new problems, such as toxic chemicals generated by industrial processes. But, on balance, technology is a potent life-enhancing force. It has made life richer, longer, and more free of pain than ever before. Romantic fascination with the past can be sustained only at the cost of invincible historical ignorance.

Such ignorance is promoted even by the celebrated "live" educational exhibits of history. Colonial Williamsburg, for example, has a unique opportunity to show daily life in Jefferson's and Washington's day. Yet visitors to the restored city see neatly kept houses, clean streets, and newly made furniture of old design. Air-conditioned restaurants serve wholesome food prepared in immaculate kitchens.

Is this how it used to be? I doubt that the smells of the old city could be reproduced; if they could, tourists would leave at once. Food was cooked in filthy kitchens, guest rooms were infested with roaches, and rats and mice roamed the unpaved streets. Nearly all the inhabitants carried parasites, many died young, and most of those past thirty suffered from severe dental problems and gum disease. The world then was a dirty and dangerous place in which people were rarely safe from illness and almost never comfortable.

If that be wholesome life, give me chemicals and air-conditioning and, by all means, instant communication with my loved ones far away. If a machine could take our romantics back in time, they would beg to return to the safety and comfort of our civilized ways. The closest we can actually come to time travel is a trip to some less developed corner of the globe. So let those who wish to condemn the benefits of technology live for an experimental year or two in a primitive village near the end of the road. Would they not wish to come back at the end of the first week? The vast majority even of those who enjoyed their Peace Corps experiences were delighted to return to civilization.

To love life is to love all the good things it offers. The marvelous new products and stunning opportunities of industrial, and now information-based, society are among the best of these. To go for a week to Hawaii may seem hedonistic, and to fly over the South Pole has been called superficial. But they are experiences ordinary people could never have had before. They are exciting and enriching and enjoyable; do those who stay home profit more? I celebrate the modern world in all its glory, with all its machines, its conveniences and its comforts. To love life is to drink up all of it, to do it all, to hug it as our own.

Sometimes the attack on modern life masquerades as a sort of spirituality. But such holiness can define itself only by the war it wages on convenience. There is a deep undercurrent of such feeling among intellectuals who declare the goods of industrial society, our opportunity-enhancing machines, and the fineries of life unnecessary, even wicked luxuries. In their attack on the benefits of technology, however, they never explain where to draw the line. If electronic mail is harmful to the soul, are letters also if they move by truck? Is there something wholesome in communicating by smoke signals that is lost when we turn to CNN? If dishwashers are unnecessary, shall we abandon soap as well, and clean water later in the year?

The truth is that religion does not forbid us to live well. In his great work on religious experience, the American philosopher William James wrote, "life, more life, a larger, richer, more satisfying life, is, in the last analysis, the end of religion. The love of life…is the religious impulse." Sensible people enjoy life in all its pleasures and helpful products. Without ideological baggage, we choose every convenience we can afford and embrace every life-improving, opportunity-creating invention.

Life really is much better today than it was even a hundred years ago, partly because we have learned greater respect for our bodies and take better care of them. We have also developed marvelous devices that enable us to do with ease what we could never have done before. Not only are we in love with life; life now is more worthy of our love.

Wanting More Life

Not the least, loving life means wanting more of it. Dread of death is not the outcome, as the poet Walt Whitman thought, of imagining the world going on in our absence. It is rather the unspeakable grief of having to cease the activities we so enjoy. The dying we do in the process of aging is just such a surrender of activities: little by little we become unable to do the things we like. Death in its finality just completes this retreat, closing the door on all voluntary activities.

To want more life is, therefore, to want not the blank of mere biological survival, but rather a continuing sequence of things we can do and achievements we can enjoy. Even for those unattracted to infinite Faustian craving, the appetite for activity feeds on itself and lifts only slowly with the loss of energy in the last season of life. Nothing shows the importance of doing things more than the difficult idea of heaven. What would it be like to spend endless time in a place where everything is right? What would we do eon after eon? We recoil with horror at the idea that our only activity would be to sing the praises of the Lord. With *my* voice, day after day, unto eternity?

Holding onto life can be the pathetic expression of fear. But normally, it is the lusty sign of an uncompleted agenda or of a surfeit of energy. Like a person struck by a bullet who continues to charge ahead, the momentum of life carries us along. The eighty-year-old who persists in traveling because there is so much to see and the cancer-riddled mother who refuses to die because there is a child to raise serve as exemplars of what it means to want more life and why. They and the rest of us keep moving because important things remain to be thought and said and felt and seen and done.

An elderly man once started coming to my classes. At lunch, Bob told me that he had recently sold the store to which he had devoted his life. He said that, at seventy-two, he felt he had not lived at all. Over the following years, he threw himself into activities for which he had not had the time or money before. He took college classes, went on a long trip to China, and developed a circle of friends with whom he could discuss economics and history. He and his wife traveled to Europe several times to see what life there was like and what centuries of faith had built. Over what became regular lunches, he told me what he was thinking and what new things he had learned. The world was a new and wonderful place for this man who had lived long but was not old.

Bob's first bout with cancer was a war. He vowed to beat the disease and cheerfully submitted to every invasive treatment his doctors recommended. I admired him for his un-complaining fortitude. And he was rewarded with several more years of travel and friendship, even though in a weak-ened condition. Then the cancer returned and Bob was no longer willing to fight. His friends urged him on: another operation and more chemotherapy might yield six more months of life, perhaps a year. I was disappointed in his de-cision to fight no more. I could not understand how some-one who had been so full of life could ever call it quits.

Only long reflection on Bob made me realize what an important lesson he had taught me. He was in love with life and he was willing to fight for his love. But one must not want anything at all costs; sometimes the price is too high for what you get. The first course of treatments had weak-ened him; the second would have made most of the activi-ties he enjoyed impossible. Travel would have had to be given up, and the cancer, growing at the mouth of the stomach, would have made lunches with friends an embar-rassing torture. Bob had had enough. A few more months of life confined to a room or bed could not justify the suf-fering and the sense of loss.

The lesson is clear. Love life so long as there is something worth loving; for most of us, just breathing for another year is not. As we age or suffer from disease, we learn to sacrifice a lot for diminishing returns. So long as we can continue to do and feel and think and say, it is foolish to give up. But at some point, wanting more life runs into the chill reality that the kind of life we can get is no longer worth the cost. This does not mean that we surrender our love of life. As in a broken love affair, we give up the loved one, not the love. With anguish or with quiet resignation, we face the fact that the days of love are gone.

2

Hating Life

Hating All Life?

Some people claim to hate life. There is nothing surprising about this. Children sometimes trample on ants, and adults act like artists with the fly swatter. But such activities are not motivated by hatred of life in a general way, only dislike of some bit of life or of an annoying creature. People terminate such lives without a second thought, not out of malice but as a game or as an indication of low esteem.

From time to time, we also hate our own lives or some element of them. So I may abhor my circumstances, if long hours of work rob me of the opportunity to find love. Or I might despise my molars because they make me transfer a large part of my paycheck to the dentist. But this is not hatred of life either. The hate is based on love: what makes for the dislike is that its object interferes with our getting enough of what we want.

Hating Life

The man who, knowing he suffered from AIDS, proceeded to have unprotected sex with a string of women and men presents a more interesting case of hatred of life. The motive seemed to be resentment of bad luck or at least the desire to spread his misforturne as broadly as possible. But the focus of the hatred is revealing. The sick man did not throw his blood in the eyes of passers-by; as if he wanted to punish them, he restricted his venom to those who would share his bed. So even this is not a case of general hatred of life but of special anger over something, directed at a few individuals.

Hatred, like all human responses, is easy to generalize. Those who walk into McDonald's or up in the bell tower to shoot as many people as they can, do not mean to limit their victims to any special group. They are indiscriminate and inclusive, prepared to shoot anyone and, if they could, everyone. Their dislike for humans is so great that they see no reason to hold back whenever even innocent strangers can be hurt. Although the hatred such people feel is remarkably broad, it is still a long way from being universal. For one thing, they don't hate themselves to the point of doubting their own judgment of the worthlessness of others. Moreover, transferring their allegiance from humans to animals, many of them develop tender relations with their pets. Their own justification for loathing humanity is not that all life is rotten to the core, but that humans represent a particularly degraded form of life.

The view that human life is worthless is particularly attractive to those who wish to abuse it or to use it for their own benefit. Yet the murderer Jeffrey Dahmer and others like him never seem to spend much time considering the possibility that *no* human life is of value; they are satisfied that they, at least, are of sufficient excellence to justify having others die for them. They face, therefore, the moral problem of selfishness, which is how one can justify radically better treatment for oneself than for others. One source of their selfishness is what William James called "a certain blindness": a lack of ability to imagine the inner life of another, that is, to experience in their minds what it feels like to be one of their victims.

The person in my own experience who came closest to hatred of all life was a rough-hewn man, perhaps forty years old, whose front teeth were missing. His muscular body was covered with tattoos, many of which he inflicted himself. He explained gleefully that he enjoyed being a tattoo artist because he liked nothing better than "dealing pain." He viewed his entire existence as focused on making life squirm, on causing as much pain as possible to everyone, including himself.

At first, I was impressed by the man's steadfast commitment not to exclude himself from the punishment he thought all life deserved. But as he spoke about how much he liked inflicting and suffering pain, I realized that, in one important respect at least, he was no enemy of life. His intense eyes and the excitement in his voice betrayed how very much he was in love with his life and with his odd, distorted values. He was so focused on torturing life that he never noticed the joy such torture gives.

Such intensification of life in the face of danger, suffering, and death is the nearly universal experience of those at war. In times of struggle, the threat of annihilation and the excitement of causing it make every moment of existence vivid and memorable. Fifty years after World War II, combatants still maintained that, throughout it, they had had an unrivaled sense of being alive. Forgetting the misery, many of them wished they could recapture the magic just once more. They loved life then with a passion that flows only from risk and imminent death. Their job, as soldiers, was to destroy people, but energy is irrepressible even when directed against itself. Hating and killing life make us love our own existence all the more.

Universal hatred of life seems, then, to be beyond our power. The hostility we feel focuses our energy and makes us experience our destructive efforts as exciting and worthwhile. The enemies of existence, therefore, love themselves while they loathe many, most, or all others. Their sustained animosity toward other people depends on their ability to draw a clear line between themselves and the rest of the world. Once that line is breached by seeing others as similar to themselves, their love of life can spread to fill the reach of the imagination.

Indifference to Life

Some people cannot summon the energy it takes to hate life. They operate on a low budget of vitality, as if their psychic metabolism required little nourishment and yielded only feeble output. One can think of a mushy handshake as the symbol of this attitude to life: such individuals seem to attack the problems of existence with the vigor of Jell-O. Their eyes don't flash and they rarely grit their teeth; their anger is subdued and their voice is dull and low. Tasks loom in front of them like impassable mountains, so they feel defeated before they start.

In Love with Life

Individuals who are low spirited about everything or nearly everything tend to be relatively invisible. Some hold insignificant jobs while others remain in the care of their families, or of institutions, all their lives. Their low achievements are both the cause and the outcome of their low self-esteem. After repeated failures, they may simply quit trying and surrender all significant purposeful activity. I have seen a few people reach this level of human motionlessness or vegetation: it may take them an hour to build up to having breakfast and two or three weeks to open the mail.

Fortunately, very few people decay to this state of inactivity. Temporary medical conditions, such as mononucleosis, reduce some to suspended animation; others go through a stage of vacant staring as a result of depression or disappointed love. But most of those who reach the bottom bounce back and begin to taste the pleasures of life again. This happens in the regular course of events, suggesting that engagement with the world and enjoyment of that engagement are natural to humans in reasonable health.

Another sort of indifference infects those whose lives are uniform to the point of monotony. This regularity is the outcome of momentum, not of the passion for orderliness that attempts to organize everything down to the minutest detail. The momentum derives from need or social circumstance and is carried by inert habit. Such people keep doing what they have always done. They do it not altogether mechanically, but without much variation and without zest or appetite. To them, life is a dull set of requirements to which one cheerlessly submits. Their indifference is not deliberate. It does not result from a thoughtful assessment of human prospects, but from a quiet sense that life is nothing much and then we die.

This feeling of cosmic gloom has a social counterpart. Both government and the institutions with which we deal and in which we work have become gigantic. Individuals, by contrast, have been reduced to easily replaced functionaries or role players in the vast social apparatus that sustains modern life. All of us experience our insignificance in society. All of us know what it means to feel powerless at a time of great social changes or against mighty institutions. Some rebel against these limits of individual life, while others make their peace the way the oboe must to remain in the orchestra. A few, however, feel crushed and live permanent defeat. Their indifference is that of beaten slaves, expressing hopelessness but also serving as a shield against disappointment.

The social system not only crushes individuals but also uses them up. We see young people rushing in to be high-powered lawyers, traders, and executives, only to have the life sucked out of them by the demands of their jobs. Their excitement and their excellence carry them far up the ladder of success until, usually all at once, they seem to run out of energy and caring. Some realize that their work will never leave them time for satisfactions and responsibilities they consider vital. Others see their families walk out on them, or lose their health and turn with resentment against the pressures of competing that, they think, caused their ruin. A few simply burn out and see no point in going on.

These dropouts from the fast track are all around us. Most of them recycle their skills and find modest objectives to pursue. No one on the outside can know the condition of their souls. Do they reach happiness at last, or do they grieve the loss of their day in the sun?

Some of those who leave the world of ambition never regain their energy. A student of mine many years ago rushed through school to bring the world to its knees. He called me often to tell me with delight how quickly he was rising to the top at the large corporation where he worked. He became the youngest vice president in the history of the company and was groomed to be the boss. Then suddenly, before he could capture the prize, he quit his job. He spent the next nine months visiting old friends, as if he had unfinished business left over from his youth. He came to see me, but he had nothing to say. He appeared distant from everything and indecisive. He wanted neither to stay overnight nor to leave; he didn't care to discuss where he had come from and was unconcerned about where he would go. I have never heard from him again. The life that had burnt so brightly in him had been extinguished, and nothing seemed to matter any more.

The types of indifference of which I have so far spoken are outcomes of personal inclination or experience. Another sort results from deliberate effort. Its achievement is a triumph of self-discipline, turning energy against itself until desire and spontaneous delight are stilled. Stoic philosophers during the days of the Roman Empire and their many followers since then made an art of such self-control, teaching themselves to overcome fear, love, concern, and longing—everything that might perturb their peace of mind. As a result, the Stoics were able to stop caring about the course of the world: their indifference to everything that happens has become legendary in the history of the West.

Hating Life

The insight that motivates stoics is recognition of human weakness. The power any individual can wield is insignificant when compared to the might of society or nature. The cooperative efforts of the entire human race can be rubbed out by a relatively small increase in the average temperature of the earth, and all the monuments of our creativity might well be obliterated by a comet that strays off course.

At the very least, each of us is certain to die, and prior to death to suffer pain and loss. There is simply nothing we can do about this, except to try to put off the moment of reckoning. Even that delay is ultimately not within our power: some cannot die when they want, while others perish desperate for life. Human power is so circumscribed that it is best to acknowledge impotence and lay up our treasures in another place.

The "other place" for stoics is not a heaven distant from here, but the narrow sphere over which each of us has perfect control. This is the realm of our feelings and attitudes which, they optimistically believe, we can always adjust. The right way to adjust them is to bring them in line with reality, so that by expecting and accepting misfortune we can escape its sting. Life is a chain of problems, so we are born into trouble: easily injured from conception on, we make ourselves even more vulnerable by emotional attachments to persons and possessions.

Yet in historical perspective, our concerns look petty; from the standpoint of the birth of stars or even the development of the earth, they are infinitely small. People who understand this realize how little our problems matter and how insignificant we are. If we remain steadfast in the belief that in the end nothing really matters, we can achieve a tranquillity that makes existence worthwhile.

The stoic's indifference is, therefore, a conscious strategy to achieve peace of mind. Epictetus the slave and Marcus Aurelius the Roman emperor agree that because these are dangerous emotions, life is to be neither loved nor hated. We must simply take it as it comes. When it favors us, there is little reason to rejoice because, quite likely, soon it won't. If it crushes us, there is no reason to complain: since we know we are mortal, it should not surprise us that we die. All we can hope to get from life is an understanding of how things really are and the quiet satisfaction that attends facing the greatest tragedies with total calm.

The steely resolve of stoics is admirable and may, in fact, be just the right attitude in times of trouble. Yet I cannot help thinking that equanimity, precious as it is, stands in the way of getting the most out of life. Indifference of all sorts makes life dull. The sweet glow of youth, the intensity of desire and love, and the exhilaration of success are among the best reasons to live. If we give up all of this, if we refuse to enjoy the excitement of the explosive energy that drives us, there is not much left. Of course, reaching makes us vulnerable, and then it is only a matter of time before we get hurt. But we will be hurt whether we strive or not, so it makes good sense to feel the power while we can and let tranquillity wait until we're old.

Why Hate Life?

Why should anyone hate *life*? Consider the alternative. For anyone not totally convinced that we are immortal, death is not an attractive prospect. By comparison with utter nonbeing, even relatively miserable lives display some redeeming features. A flash of joy here and there goes a long way toward making an existence that is not rent by permanent anxiety or racked by pain worthwhile. Why, then, find fault with what may well be the source or condition of our only satisfaction and our only hope?

Some people hate life on principle: they detest the fact that it falls short of the ideal. This means that reality fails to come up to their expectations or, as I have heard it from some utopians, that it would take only ten minutes to think up a world vastly better than this. Such an ideal system of life need not be perfect in every particular, they say, but it would have to be free at least of the most egregious injustice and suffering. And once we begin to think about it, why stop there? If there is to be a world at all, it should be as good as possible. Going by that standard, the cruel and confusing world we live in does not rate at all.

The struggle with this awful realization has occupied theologians for thousands of years. Why would a God of unlimited power and wisdom create such a flawed universe? How can a Being of infinite goodwill let the suffering go on? The most infuriating answer the theologians have offered is that all this supposed evil is not real. Can we believe this when we look at a child dying of cancer, in great pain? Another favorite answer, that the suffering is necessary to make the world perfect, is transparently sophistical. Is a perfection that does not require such misery not better than one that does? The best response by far comes from pious believers who admit that it is hopeless to try to understand. Faith in a supreme creator leaves us in the position of Job, humbled and admiring the greatness but unable to comprehend.

Those who hate the world because of its imperfection do not suffer from an excess of humility. They claim to know how it could be better, and they are convinced that they would have made it better had they been in charge. They are certainly right that we can imagine all sorts of adjustments to how things are that would decrease the amount and intensity of pain. If only no child were born deformed, if only we did not age into disease and idiocy, if only we were not ravaged by such ailments as cancer and diabetes, we would all find life more satisfying. We *can* come up with such imaginary improvements all day long. The problem is that they are fictive, more like the daydreams of children than the standards by which sober people can judge.

Are we to hate life because it is not as good as it could be? Should we send back the meal because the rice is turning cold? It might be better to warm the rice with the sauce and enjoy our good fortune in having food and company. There is something of the spoiled child in the demand that everything be just so or we will not play. The way we find the world is not optional: that is the great given in our lives. And the only time life will seem perfect is when we lose our dreams. But no matter how bad the world is, it is also good; and however many people add to its misery, it is also open to being made a little better. The greatest danger for those in love with the ideal is that they make the best the enemy of the good.

People of particularly tender feelings go a step further, however, and condemn life for what may be its most pervasive characteristic. There is something unspeakably cruel about the fact that we must eat to live and that living creatures must die so we may eat. This structural feature of life suggests something more sinister than failure to live up to our ideals. Schopenhauer thought that the horror of the food chain points to an element of the diabolical in the world and could serve as an argument that the Devil is the lord of creation. He was convinced that the suffering of animals amounts to an ineradicable moral stain on life, showing that existence, maintained at the expense of others, is utterly unjustifiable.

This is a powerful condemnation. If life were just imperfect, it might be a matter of individual choice whether we wished to participate. But if every minute of one's joy is bought with the blood and death of someone else, the entire enterprise is rotten to the core. Choosing life under these circumstances makes us complicit in the pain; enjoying it shows an abhorrent lack of moral sensitivity. According to this view, we end with no choice but to cut our lives short in order to extend the lives of others.

Like so many striking moral arguments, this bit of reasoning suffers from exaggeration. The food chain has its horrors, but the misery is nowhere near universal. The majority of plants live on sunlight and inanimate materials. Moreover, we can hardly charge animals that eat plants with the destruction of conscious, feeling life. That leaves carnivores with the moral burden of having to kill to eat. Although humans have a choice in the matter, being able to get by as vegetarians, most animals don't. If killing is the problem, they are therefore faced with a hideous dilemma: they either destroy others to eat or destroy themselves by not eating. This is a moral problem to which there is no good solution; we are stuck in the given with no room to maneuver.

Is this awful feature of some animal life enough to justify general hatred of existence? Interestingly enough, any hatred it legitimates depends on love. If life were not something wonderful and precious, killing to eat would be of no moral significance. The food chain appears so horrible because we love life and suppose that all animals do, and because we think pain is a great obstacle to the enjoyment of life and suppose that all animals think so too. Without this love, we would have no reason to hate; we hate life only because it does not allow all to love and to enjoy it in peace forever. But does it make sense to swear eternal hate because, at some point in the night, our lover whispers "Enough"?

Beyond these general causes of anger, those who hate life have private grievances. There are ample reasons for such complaints: fate has dealt a poor hand to many. Some are born crippled, diseased, or predisposed to chronic ailments; others suffer the misfortune of growing up in broken or abusive homes. Some people are irredeemably stupid, while others bear the curse of stunning ugliness. Disaster strikes some individuals savagely in mid-career, as it did a friend whose muscles that lift the eyelids started to atrophy. Soon he could no longer open his eyes and now lives, with 20/20 vision, in the dark.

Only those who have not suffered or who lack the blessings of imagination fail to sympathize with such bad luck. The rest can understand the bitterness of the afflicted, their anger at their condition and at the world that caused it or permitted it to come about. But do such people truly despise life? I suspect they hate only their own and look with envy at what they think is the problem-free existence of everyone else. And probably they do not dislike everything even about their own lives, reserving negative feelings mainly for their problems or lamentable condition.

The extent to which hatred of their own situation makes them hate all of life is a good measure of how much they think the universe revolves around them. Those who believe they inhabit only a small corner of the world do not let their problems poison the beauty around them. They take pleasure in seeing how good life can be, even if its beneficiaries are mainly others. In contrast, individuals whose misfortune colors their perception of reality cannot avoid thinking of themselves as central in the scheme of things. Where we situate the self and how we draw its periphery become, in this way, critical issues in whether we love or hate the world.

Limits of Self

Biology forms the basis of our overwhelming concern for ourselves. Personhood is connected to the life and fortunes of the body: the fact that the organism is a free-standing sensor and agent serves as the foundation of the old wisdom that we all suffer our own pains and die our own deaths. When I cut my finger, my loved ones do not bleed. I may experience the deepest sorrow over the suffering of a good friend, but I cannot shoulder his pain. We appear to be cut off, therefore, from the rest of the world by the architecture of our being. The self seems confined to a tiny island whose welfare it must guard and whose destiny it shares. The island is surrounded by a bottomless sea, so our isolation is complete: no one can visit and we cannot leave.

Some philosophers have thought that this splendid isolation justifies, even requires, selfishness. As a result, they have developed various theories of egoism, claiming that no sound account of values can start anywhere but in the imperative of looking out for number one. These theories thrive, even seem compelling, in times of social upheaval and to individuals at odds with their society. A feeling of rightness seems to pervade them, and holding them gives tough-minded people the sense that they strike a blow against the tender foolishness of morality.

Powerful as the picture of the lone animal may be, the image of insularity is severely misleading. The islands we think we are have submerged connections with the mainland. The sand, the rocks, all the contents of our selves speak of external origin: however individual, even unique and spectacular, we may think ourselves, we are to a substantial extent products of our society. The most individualistic Americans are easily recognized as Americans everywhere in the world, perhaps precisely because they are so careful to be individualistic.

The moral problem, however, relates not to the origin but to the extension of the self. Here again we see that biology is not determinative. Social life builds on physical abilities and predispositions as if on a platform; the resulting constructions reveal only the most general features of the foundation. In some cultures, for example, it would not occur to people to think of themselves as persons separate from their family or tribe. In others, people view themselves as continuous with the flow of life in everything that moves.

Such perceptions and commitments, and the practices that flow from them, do not rise to the surface from the depths of our physiology. They are expressions of the historical and cultural context in which we grow up and operate. Our activities, the values by which we live and for which we die, even the way we feel about things, are the products largely of social factors.

This suggests that the scope of the self is at least partly the outcome of choice and is, therefore, adjustable. We see evidence that it has undergone evolutionary growth in the history of humankind. The great psychologist and philosopher William James has shown convincingly that it ranges in extent from the most private element in our souls to the entire human race.

Few people would not consider their bodies parts of themselves. But many go beyond that and view their parents, mates, and children, their beloved dogs and cats, even their clothes and cars as vital elements of who they are: threats or damage to any of these make them fight just as fiercely as if someone had punched them in the nose. Since what I think of as mine can quickly become a part of me, my friends and family, my church, club, and community are all normally incorporated into the economy of my self. An insult to my country turns, in this way, into an insult to me, and litter on the street is removed with the same readiness and for the same reason as garbage in the living room.

To be sure, many people don't extend their sense of self to anywhere near this point. But the history of civilization coincides precisely with the gradual expansion of the boundaries of the self. We have learned to see first others close to us, then anonymous members of our group, eventually our enemies, and finally, in a halting way, the multitude of strangers that constitute humankind as somehow vitally involved in who we are. Only such extended ego-boundaries can explain why industrial nations offer helping hands when disaster strikes on the other side of the globe. We can see self-interest as the source of foreign aid, of peacekeeping missions, and of humanitarian help only if we think in terms of such an enlarged notion of self.

Expanding the scope of who and what is involved in our existence is essential for love of life. Most of those who hate life despise it not on principle but because of how it has treated them. If they could think of themselves not as narrowly confined in stunted bodies or as struck by private disaster, they might be able to reduce their anger and their hate.

Somewhere around us, life is always in flower; if we can focus on that and see it as our own, a measure of delight can take the place of pain. We do this routinely in viewing sports events. The speed and strength and skill we observe evoke pleasure and admiration rather than envy or resentment. The successes of scientists, engineers, and doctors, the achievements of painters and dancers—vitality and power wherever we find them—make us fall in love with life again.

If the private self suffers disaster, it is best to expand its boundaries past the distress. Hatred of life is then dissolved in a greater movement, in the vibrancy and the fresh victories that surround us on all sides. This is the reason why isolated retirement communities and nursing homes face the danger of becoming sad, bitter places.

In separating the old from the normal activities of life, we condemn them to mourning their decline. In exile from the energy that propels the world, they cannot take solace in seeing, as aging football players do, that the game goes on. Distant from the young, their memories are not lush celebrations of the past reborn, but the rustle of dry leaves. They miss the great vision of the continuity of life and the indestructibility of energy. They die before they die because their fire is gone out and they cannot warm themselves at someone else's hearth.

We face no danger, therefore, that in enjoying life we shall neglect our obligations. On the contrary, doing what we must can itself be a joyous celebration of control over self and of our connectedness. Since the bulk of the moral life consists in giving the good of others equal consideration with our own, seeing ourselves as at one or at least as continuous with our neighbors helps us fulfill its demands. The expansion of ego-boundaries that has been the aim of civilization all along reduces wickedness as it enhances joy in life. Responding to the needs of others and delighting in their good fortune are but two sides of the same striking growth of humanity.

3

The Rat Race

Overdrive

Imagine a world in which life is not vibrant. The seeds of plants lie lazily in the sun; instead of springing up and eagerly colonizing every inch of usable ground, they grow sluggishly even in the best soil. Birds don't sing in the morning, and animals mate reluctantly and only on rare occasions. Parents grieve the birth of sons and daughters, and children don't frolic, sitting gloomily, tired eyes staring into the distance. Human life proceeds without excitement and without the great epidemics of feeling we see in desire and in love. There is little drive and no competition because, without ambition and energy, doing anything at all feels like too much trouble.

Perhaps we view such a world as sad and unredeemed only because we feel driven by the energy of life. Given who we are, however, it is difficutlt to see much of value in a wilted universe. Even those among us who seek inner peace do so with intensity. When the profound Danish philosopher Kierkegaard declares that purity of heart is to will one thing, he means that we must will it with passion and total devotion. Many of our ideas of heaven center on the success of our activities, not on their absence: in thinking that in such a future state we might have but the single, simple task of chanting the praises of the Lord, we assume without question that we will sing vigorously and well. We think of life without energy as lost on the road from the pitiful to the horrid.

We pay a high price for this infatuation with energy. Like an engine with open throttle, it can hurtle us to our graves. Unsated drives can become insatiable. If they take over our lives, we work without end and never allow ourselves the satisfaction of thinking that we have accomplished anything worthwhile. The magnitude and multitude of tasks come to dwarf everything we achieve, and we forget that these high demands are compelling only because our will fastens on them and won't let them go. Intellectually, the result is the view that no matter how much we do, we are always guilty, that in effect we can never do enough. Believing such things makes people emotional wrecks.

Operating in overdrive is a problem not restricted to individuals. It has been institutionalized in the ways industrialized societies function. Life in such high-pressure environments is often viewed as a rat race. The reference is to luckless creatures caught on a treadmill of repetitive, meaningless routines. Many people feel that, like such rodents, they perform insignificant activities to gain ends that ultimately fail to satisfy. Yet they do them, out of habit or necessity, and impotently watch their best years disappear.

The rat race is a struggle for success and money. We enter it because we have ambitions and needs. These desires are strong enough to seem to enslave us by tying us to a cycle of actions that lead nowhere we want to be. The activities are, for the most part, valuable only for what they yield; they are of little worth in their own right. We learn to do them because without them we cannot get ahead and perhaps cannot even eat.

Both statistics and personal testimony show that many people dislike their jobs. They feel they spend a significant part of their waking hours doing mindless things, or at least things unworthy of their efforts. They think of themselves as taking a deep breath on Monday mornings and going under water, to emerge on Friday afternoons with a sigh of relief.

Others want success in a career so much that the demands of their employment take over their lives. Work expands to eighty or a hundred hours a week and displaces personal and family life. The consequences are usually ruinous, though within varied time frames: some individuals burn out quickly, others divorce, raise troubled children, or die of heart attacks. Success makes such people the envy of their fellows but earns them dissatisfaction and personal misery.

Much of our work life is unpleasant because the tasks we must undertake are boring and repetitious. Moreover, nearly all of them involve deferral, requiring that we do things for the sake of something else we want to obtain.

Life becomes, in this way, an unbroken cycle of means to other means that we hope will lead to truly desirable, though always distant, ends. We get so used to the deferral that when our aims are at last achieved, we can hardly believe it and cannot really enjoy them. So long as we keep looking to the future, satisfaction always escapes us.

People caught in the grind of daily life often ask themselves what, if anything, in their existence is worthwhile. Weekdays drag, soaked in a dismal seriousness that will not let up. Weekends disappear, leaving a hunger for play and forgetfulness. People remember childhood, even their years in school, with longing, as times of happiness never to be regained.

Lack of what satisfies profoundly drives us to seek something transcendent through religion or by other means. The sort of religion particularly attractive to people in the rat race is not focused on a set of beliefs or rituals. Its primary benefit, moreover, is not the consolation in the face of misfortune that religion frequently provides, but inner peace through escape from striving. In whatever religious language we describe this transcendence, its role is to provide something of unquestioned and immediate value in which we can rest. The peace that passes all understanding also passes all measures and means of achievement in this world.

Religious practices that would otherwise hold little attraction for Westerners acquire, in this way, a surprising crowd of adherents. People study Zen Buddhism or sign over their worldly goods to spiritual masters in order to find the elusive but all-important secret of inner peace. Although some who are devoted to televangelists seek assurance that they will never die, many others want only something un-problematic in which, as though in the bosom of Abraham, they can forget their struggles and gain release.

Much as we abominate the endless rounds of busy-ness, the rat race penetrates our lives and shapes us in its image. The daily grind comes to define who we are and to set the aims and limits of existence. The thought that our situation cannot be changed quickly moves us from resistance to ac-ceptance, and we find ourselves viewing the dull repetitions of daily life as natural. Nothing is better evidence of this than the aimlessness of the retired. Having at last escaped the need to do what they'd rather not, simply to make a liv-ing, many of them tend to lose all appetite and interest in life. The release they enjoy is also a letting go, but without rudder and engine they languish and then die.

Making Means Meaningful

Why must all enjoyments be bought with hard labor? Why should a chain of painful conditions or preliminaries precede each brief moment of joy? Common sense is satu-rated with the recognition that life is a mixed bag. We say that into each life some rain must fall and that we have to take the good with the bad. But we go well beyond the idea that pain and pleasure go together and think that one is the price we pay for the other. There is after all, we keep re-minding ourselves, no free lunch; we have to pay our dues and work for everything we get.

Things might not go this way in an ideal world, though we would have to reside in an ideal world already to agree about what is ideal. Here, what some consider the slavery of their jobs is built on the universal need to sustain life. When Adam and Eve were banished from the Garden of Eden, God condemned them to earn their living by the sweat of their brows.

This represents a painful insight into the condition of humans and of animals generally. Life is constantly running down: the food we eat is soon used up, and without sleep attention idles and then dies. We must protect ourselves from the elements and renew life at every turn. The renovation of the body requires ceaseless effort; chipmunks and chickadees seem to get hardly more energy from the food they eat than it takes them to gather it.

The drive to adjust conditions of nature so that they support human flourishing has led to the development of vast systems of production and distribution. But increasing ease in obtaining the necessities of life has not liberated us from work and care. Needs expand to keep pace with the availability of goods: we learn to want only chicken breast and steak, to convert the requirement of transportation into a demand for fancy cars. The rewards of the industrial world impel us, in this way, into voluntary bondage. We work longer hours than our hungry ancestors and take less time and energy to enjoy the fruits of our labor.

If a command economy forced us to work day and night, resistance would be easy. No one can police the carelessness or contrived incompetence of masses of people. We could drag our feet and chortle over how well we sabotage the system. But our compulsion comes from inside, making individuals the custodians and judges of their efforts. They become merciless masters, driving themselves as one drives slaves into whatever activity seems needed to attain their goals.

In Love with Life

There is no escaping the internal gaze that risks sharpening the competitive impulse into an instrument of self-destruction. The ruin can be physical, crushing the body under the stress created by myriad tasks and endless expectations. It can be psychological, burning up the circuitry of motivation and flinging people of high promise under bridges and into the streets to finish their lives as bums or derelicts. It can also be personal, robbing individuals of satisfaction and reducing their lives to meaningless strife and stifling routine. Often, persons of means attain their wealth by exclusive attention to the means, allowing their broader human ends to slip from sight. The rat race has more casualties than a war.

Are there ways to escape a life in which the struggle for the conditions of happiness makes attaining happiness impossible? Can we overcome what feels like slavery to an endless cycle of means so we can savor our satisfying ends? Philosophers have suggested two approaches to lifting the burden of unrewarding activities. John Dewey and others who focus on community life call for social changes to eliminate the rat race. Stoics, on the other hand, recommend psychological renewal to alter our relationship to what we cannot avoid doing. A judicious combination of the two can bring us close to a satisfying life.

Some jobs demand mainly repetitive and personally meaningless activities. People who wash hair, fill gas tanks, or inspect cigarettes as they move down a conveyor belt may find it difficult to avoid boredom. They cannot bolster their self-respect by reminding themselves of the importance of their tasks, and they cannot pretend that what they do is novel enough to present a challenge.

The Rat Race

The only hope, therefore, is that the world might get along without humans having to do such things. And, indeed, the development of technology has transferred many jobs unfit for us to computers and heavy machinery. We do not dig ditches by hand any more and the days at the telephone company when thousands spent their lives connecting calls while thousands of others sorted long distance tickets are happily over.

Some recurring tasks, however, cannot or should not be transferred to machines. Much learning and the development of nearly all skills involves potentially boring repetition. We cannot master the piano without extensive practice or become historians without reading a large number of books that detail the same events. And although we could change all communication with banks and other businesses to punching numbers into a computer, it is desirable to retain an element of human contact even at the cost of such tedious jobs as teller and receptionist.

The key to dealing with this problem is to arrange tasks in such a way that we can retain our interest while performing them. Learning occurs more rapidly, for example, when students are alert. This argues for a shift in our educational system. We need to reduce forced repetition and find ways to stimulate the attention and imaginative playfulness of students.

The growing conviction that we should teach young people the "basics" gets confused in many minds with the idea that we should teach them in the painful and inept way we ourselves were taught. Drills to achieve a hundred multiplications in three minutes add little to understanding and a great deal to the lifelong hatred of math. Teachers who present multiplication as a set of interesting relations, instead, and show its relevance to vital concerns of life do not have to struggle against tides of indifference on the shoreline of sleep.

The best thing to do with boring jobs is to avoid asking people to hold them too long or exclusively. A bit of imagination would allow rotation of positions in corporations so everyone could try writing up orders or answering the phone. The tedious daily job of one person can be a fun challenge to people elsewhere in the company. Even occasional relief from routine can make life richer for a person caught in some dead-end line of work. We don't *have* to construct lifetime jobs out of necessary tasks; the activities can be shared by everyone, or assignments to the position can be viewed as temporary, leading after a while to some other employment.

Doing the same thing and only one thing all one's life may well be the greatest obstacle to happiness in our society. Much of our educational system aims at preparing people for their ultimate occupation. The comfort and inertia of competence keep us confined to it. Change involves risk to self and family, and even those willing to assume it find they cannot be hired without experience yet cannot gain experience without being hired.

The social gains from making career changes relatively easy would vastly outweigh the costs. Even dutiful people tire of old tasks and then start slipping in performance. New challenges revitalize. At the very least, encouraging change would leave us with fewer burnt-out teachers, resentful salespeople, and washed up middle managers.

But since large-scale social adjustments come slowly, we

must convince at least ourselves that our first occupation need not be our last. Approaching work in an experimental spirit, and testing to see if it satisfies, yields greater control over life. Believing that changes may have to be made, combined with joyous acceptance of the risks involved, creates a sense of the open-endedness and excitement of existence. The exhilarating feeling that we don't know what will happen tomorrow and can't wait for the morning to come is a sign that we are totally in love with life.

Some who fear or cannot afford to risk change of employment get a second job for variety. People deskbound all day seek physically demanding work at night; those who earn their living by talk want something to occupy their hands. Even without being paid for it, other individuals throw themselves into activities distant from their jobs to allay the effects of the rat race on their souls. Many do this, perhaps without fully understanding why, through devotion to religion, to volunteer work, or to hobbies. The time expended on such endeavors may be less than we spend at work, but its intensity is considerably greater. We do these things for their own sake, and that is precisely why they satisfy.

Absorbed in Activity

Stoics are not much interested in social changes. They think the drama of our struggle for meaning is staged in the individual soul. To avoid the pointlessness of a life spent in pursuit of externalities, of things whose value resides in what they can get us, we must change our desires and attitudes.

Some of the things we do are by nature not means to further goods: we perform such activities for their own sake, with no interest in what else they yield. I might enjoy walking, for example, quite independently of its benefits for health, or seeing beautiful things without the urge to own them. If we could generalize such attitudes, stoics argue, life would consist of moments of unperturbed contentment.

Of course, stoics know that human beings cannot fully accomplish this. So they also advise indifference to what we must do but cannot change into immediately meaningful acts. But the unconcern is defensive, for positive meaning in life comes from our self-control in being able to convert obnoxious means into intrinsically enjoyable ends.

This strategy can work remarkably well. Fishing when the fish don't bite annoys people who want only to haul them in. It becomes enjoyable the moment they attend to baiting and casting and reeling in the line with no attention to the result. Conversation turns into delight in proportion to our readiness to give up such extraneous goals as making ourselves look good and convincing others to do what we want. Even playing a game is torture if our purpose is winning and not the fun of the activity.

The advantage of this gambit is that it diverts attention from the future. Life blooms in the present; the past yields shriveled, the future half-ripe fruit. Nothing satisfies but what we can embrace now, and if the hug is warm and the attention total, each moment comes alive. Celebration of the present may seem too joyous for dour stoics, yet doing things for their own sake comes to exactly that.

This celebration permits absorption in our activities without concern for motive or result. Even if only for a short time, it liberates us from anxiety by showing how delightful doing things can be. Being good at whatever we undertake enhances exhilaration, though not because it creates an exalted picture of ourselves. On the contrary, the self hardly appears at all in such focused activity. Absorption in the task is at once forgetfulness of self, which is the only way worry can be relieved.

This is the message and a good part of the reason for the attractiveness of Zen Buddhism. Oddly, humans must work hard to achieve what comes naturally to animals. We have a lot to learn from them in this regard. The way foxes stalk their prey and the abandon with which young dogs play can show us the immersion and forgetfulness we so badly need and find so difficult to attain. Deer transfixed by a scent and large birds carried on the currents of the air seem to become what they do. With no sense of past or future and no felt distinction between self and world, they live intensely for the moment and live well.

Play is a good model for understanding the delight that attends doing something for its own sake. The special attraction of many games comes from inviting or permitting self-forgetful absorption in their moves. When playfulness is not a preliminary to serious business, it creates a magical world of laughter. The play of children exhibits this sort of carefree engagement with what adults claim sadly to know as grim reality. Our lives would be better if we could follow the advice of religions and sages and learn to be childlike without becoming childish.

Making Love to Life

Unfortunately, sometimes we cannot perform the attitudinal change needed to convert painful means into joyous ends. At other times, the change gets us in trouble or simply does not work. The janitors whose lives revolve around cleaning bathrooms at the airport may not be able to view each scrubjob as intrinsically delightful. If they did, moreover, their satisfaction might add to complacency with their condition, undermining the desire to improve it. Worse, the attempt to extend the change to everything we do invites us to dote on our activities. The discipline imposed by outcomes may be a necessary check on self-indulgence.

There is a way of making life meaningful that takes this into account and works in some places where stoic transformation fails. A smooth flow of satisfactions rewards us whenever we take this route. The key consideration is that enjoyment of an event does not require forgetting about its expected outcome. On the contrary, the delight is increased if we like what we experience and believe that it will lead to other desirable things.

Reunions offer a good example. Welcoming a loved one home at the airport after a long trip is wonderful for the feelings of relief and gratitude it evokes and for the pleasure one can take in the presence of the other. The joy is intensified by the prospect of doing things together and shared laughter. Such occasions shine with both fulfillment and expectation. Their meaning resides in the entire context; in enjoying them, we embrace the moment and also its promise. To see the close connection between present delight and anticipation of the future, just consider how different the event would be if the person coming off the plane were returning home to die.

Similarly, doing well at work is gratifying both as a challenge met and as an avenue to a promotion and a good raise.

The Rat Race

Even driving a car provides the double satisfactions of moving effortlessly at high speed and of getting rapidly to where we want to be. Enjoying the same event both for what it offers in itself and for its fruits, both as end and as means, enables us to appreciate the link between present and future, enriching existence with a sense of motion and control.

Without full consciousness of what is involved, most of us agree that the best activities are those whose every element is both satisfying end and efficient means. Holding hands, for example, is delightful all by itself; but, happily, it may also persuade us to kiss. The kiss is enjoyable for just what it is; but, excitingly, it may invite the hands to explore. Every portion of the act of love as it continues is joyous, but these pleasures also build on one another and lead to each other, making for a garland of interconnected expectations and delights.

If we could treat every set of activities as such a continuous string of fulfilling-and-promising events, we would want for nothing. We could then say, by analogy, that we spent our days making love to life, kissing and caressing it as our all-satisfying lover. And we could see our actions as parts of a life-long love affair in which there is always something that gives direct delight and in which we never lack the breathless hope and sweet prospect of further consummations.

Unfortunately, converting life into love presents a variety of problems. In making love, each activity is a bit of ecstasy, and teasing deferral, impatience, and self-control constitute the only suffering. The long process of living, by contrast, has an ample share of failure and agony: we need look no further than the struggle and frustration that frame the search for love.

Worse, the means we must use to obtain our ends may be degrading or immensely painful. We may have to put up with humiliation in our jobs, a series of failures as a condition of later success, years of self-denial to pay for the schooling of children, and devastating surgery as the price of continued life. We may have to dedicate the better part of each day to menial labor, to care for a disabled mate, or to work that wrecks the body and dims the mind. Life is a fickle lover, turning away just when we most need to make love to it.

The Ideal, One Step at a Time

This makes it clear that living as though we were making love to life is an ideal. Such ideals are possibilities worth pursuing. Often, we mistakenly suppose that ideals require complete actualization, that not living up to them in any particular renders existence imperfect or the goal utopian. The error is serious because it overlooks the piecemeal nature of life and the gradualness of human improvement. These are primary realities we must acknowledge in seeking to live well.

Speaking of life in general and of the standards it should meet is a distorting abstraction. In reality, we live in specific activities one morning or one afternoon at a time. Our ideal of making *all of existence* enjoyable and productive can mean only that we try to perform *this action* in a way that is joyous and constructive—and when that is finished then the next. Since life comes in such bite-size chunks, we have a chance to set our teeth to it again and again.

What if one activity does not give the satisfaction that making love to life suggests? We can move on and try to make the next activity better. So long as we are alive, the world continues to offer new opportunities. At least some of these will let us enjoy the marvel of an act done just right that leads to the desired result. With effort and a bit of luck, the proportion of such acts may increase, enabling us to look back and say that we have had a good day or even a good year.

The focus on small achievements also helps us deal with failure. Every small accomplishment is a victory worth enjoying. The delight of the moment spreads through the body like a warm glow and boosts confidence in our ability to succeed again. The joy we feel does not report that it attends a minor triumph; it may not last long, but for a bit it colors all of life. When we fail at a small task, on the other hand, the defeat is dwarfed by contrast with our larger plans. Understood in their proper context, such frustrations invigorate; at the very least, reminders of their insignificance provide credible consolation.

Only children who don't know how the world works expect *all* of their activities to fall out right. We can live well without that, so long as we can make love to life from time to time. These moments of quiet rapture need not be acts of grand personal achievement or social import. Their significance is bounded by what we can do. For a young child, success in moving food into the mouth is victory enough, as is occasional recapture of this skill for the disoriented old. Between these two stages, life is full of small triumphs and productive delights. We go wrong when we don't enjoy them because we want more.

Measuring our condition by how much better things could be may provide motivation. But the standards we set must not be too high. Since improvement comes in small increments, imagining a vastly better world leads to paralysis of action and bitterness of soul. In times of trouble, the opposite strategy promises greater success: we need reminders that things could go much worse. Imagining ourselves crippled or fettered as slaves a thousand years ago can help restore sound judgment and our joy in life.

So even when our prospects darken, we hold the ultimate weapon. We can be grateful to be alive and we can enjoy the surge of energy in the struggle for moments of meaning and light. In this way, though we may not always make love to life or prevail over force and circumstance, we can at least glory in the effort and feel fully alive.

4

Choosing Activities

Enjoying Activities

Some of the things we do require care and attention. Planting tomatoes in the spring and controlling a car on icy roads, for example, cannot be accomplished without staying focused and alert. By contrast, we can relegate other activities to the level of habit and perform them as wonderfully elaborate, yet unreflective, routines.

Eating a sandwich and walking up a flight of stairs, for instance, are initially difficult actions that later come to demand so little thought that we can do them with casual effortlessness. Still other activities are so automatic that we are not even aware of being engaged in doing them. Heartbeat, postural changes, and adjustments of the eyes occur without effort and attention. We become conscious of them only when something goes wrong—when, for example, breathing becomes difficult or swallowing painful.

In Love with Life

The activities that constitute the physical basis of life belong to this last group. The fact that we are unaware of them unless they become a problem is the reason we typically do not enjoy our good health. We take pleasure in the physical aspect of our being when making love, working out, or playing sports, but these are not the automatic processes that sustain life. Since the activities that support life from moment to moment must be performed continuously, they sink below the level of consciousness and become difficult to retrieve. As a result, it sounds strange to suggest that we can derive pleasure from our ability to breathe or to hold ourselves erect.

Yet, upon reflection, the idea no longer seems farfetched. Sickness and health are on a par with each other in one way: part of the misery of disease is that it denies us the ability to do things we like, while health is enjoyable for the activities it makes possible. But on another level, unfortunately, the two are sharply dissimilar. We suffer intensely when we are ill, yet get little direct enjoyment out of health. There is, therefore, something unfair or unbalanced about life unless we take special measures to even the scales. We do that by learning to delight in the simple fact that we are alive.

Not surprisingly perhaps, almost everyone has such experiences of physical well-being. They capture our attention most readily upon recovery from illness. The feelings that nothing hurts any more and that the energy of life has returned can run like a warm, electric current through the body. I remember the excitement of that wave one time when, after a terrible bout with the flu, I could at last feel hunger again. The richness of my experience in eating thick pork chops with peas at a shiny diner has stayed with me for more than forty years; diners and pork chops have never ceased meaning the renewal of life to me.

Other experiences of the fullness of life can surface suddenly after physical exercise or upon waking and stretching in the morning. A hot shower can vitalize the body, and flexing muscles sometimes gives one the feeling of being intensely alive. Breathing deeply in bracing air can suddenly focus the mind on the pleasure of being able to do this simple, magnificent act. Noting the grotesqueness of how we run may give way to delighting in how muscles and bones feel when we are doing it. Those who have felt the heartbeat of an unborn child may focus with amazement and satisfaction on their own and, allowing it to fill their consciousness, achieve a sort of quiet peace.

These and other experiences give unexpected joy and put us in touch with our healthy bodies. But physical activities are by no means the only ones that offer neglected pleasures; so do elements of our mental and emotional life. Children enjoy the fun things they imagine in their daydreams. Before long, however, they begin to take delight also in their ability to dream, and construct ever fancier stories to push it to its limit.

Adults enjoy similar experiences with understanding: many of them take great satisfaction in being able to grasp how things hang together and what makes people "tick." Some individuals who have bottled up their feelings find that release of them leads to a delightfully increasing ability to experience and display emotions. And the number of times children say no reminds parents of the intense pleasures of choice and willfulness.

In Love with Life

All the fulfillments of which I have spoken so far derive simply from the exercise of our abilities. They amount to the bonus we receive from life for being active and energetic. As such, they are particularly stable and enduring. They remain available to us so long as we engage in activities, even if we are not very happy with *what* we experience or do. I can take pleasure in my ability to walk even though the neighborhood is shabby, and I can use the fact that *I* picked my investments as at least partial consolation if they lose value. Most elderly people agree that it is nice to be able to hear, even if the news is not always good.

Activities to Enjoy

In addition to enjoying our active lives, we get satisfaction also from a wide selection of specific things we do. Life consists of activities and its quality depends entirely on the choice, combination, worthiness, and success of the actions in which we engage. Unfortunately perhaps, activities involve an element of risk. Their performance requires multiple conditions, and their outcome is often in doubt.

Social life is, in part, a response to this uncertainty, offering practices and institutions to reduce risk and to make the results of human action more predictable. In industrial societies, this stabilization has been so effective that human life has come to appear secure and institutions more solid than the buildings that house them. This has made us forget the essential wisdom that the world is volatile, that life is by nature a risky adventure, and that we must exert ourselves for everything we get.

Choosing Activities

The resulting misconception can be illustrated by the difference between movie and live theater performances. Screen actors need only one fine performance: frozen on film, their actions become an enduring artifact we can inspect and enjoy. In an odd way, how Clark Gable looked and what he did in *Gone with the Wind* are still with us today.

In sharp contrast, actors in a play face a new audience each time the curtain opens and they must do once more what they have done before. No matter how well the show goes one night, it must be repeated the next, and it must be fresh and interesting again. For the actor on stage, there is no letup: the excellence of the performance dies with the night and leaves no product beyond happy memories. The energy must be renewed and spent freely so that the eight-hundredth performance of *The King and I* is as good as the best that has gone before.

That we don't see life as consisting of activities in need of constant renewal explains the failure of many human relations. Some people think of marriage, for example, as a stable structure that, once erected, requires little work or attention. They suppose that most of the effort involved comes at the front end, in courting, and that after the wedding the partners can take each other's commitment for granted.

Nothing could be further from the truth. Without continued romance, constant communication, and frequent efforts at deepening the relationship, marriages simply die. Friendships also wither unless we renew them through shared activities. Even parents who feel they have developed a satisfactory, permanent way of relating to their children may lose them if as the young people grow their elders fail to keep pace.

The moment we focus on the extent to which life consists of activities, we understand the importance of energy and the unavoidability of risk. Without energy, we are unable to perform the activities as often as we must and as well as we could. And starting with the knowledge that we may fail reduces bitterness when things don't work out.

Surprisingly, moreover, the realization that everything carries a risk can render us more experimental and bolder: it is easier to choose more risk over less than even a small chance of failure over what seems like a sure thing. As in learning to skate, the exhilaration of danger and the sense that sufficient momentum can overcome it may set us free to live with vigor and excitement.

Which activities are the best to enjoy? To questions of this sort there is no general answer. Typically, some things we do are more satisfactory than others, but so much depends on context and individual preference that universal claims should arouse suspicion. Eating is clearly better than starving to death—unless one is on a hunger strike. Making love is preferable to permanent abstinence—except for those who choose celibacy on principle or perhaps those who suffer from AIDS. Raising children is more enriching than life without them—if, that is, one has the patience, the commitment, and the means.

Human nature is so diverse that generalizations invite counterexamples and blanket prescriptions prove futile. In the place of a universal hierarchy of values, we must be satisfied with identifying the factors that affect sensible choice. Ability, opportunity, satisfaction, social standards, and variety are the five most important considerations to take into account when we choose activities to enjoy.

Ability

Individual ability establishes the parameters of action. Competitive running is beyond the reach of someone with uneven legs, as is astronomy of those whose math skills peaked at long division. But even individual limits are flexible and can be extended with training and effort. Adult illiterates may think they cannot learn to write, but a bit of trying quickly proves them wrong. And although some find taking charge of their emotions very difficult, need or embarrassment can help them gain control.

Some people accomplish less, others more than they think they can. Typically, they achieve less so long as they are governed by wishes and spend their time hoping for good things to happen. They do more when will propels them to back what they want with concentrated labor. But drive is of no avail without a shrewd assessment of what is possible.

The trick is to know where effort is likely to make a difference and how much energy to expend before calling it quits. I saw a striking demonstration of how not to do this in the behavior of a beautiful cardinal that gave new meaning to the word *birdbrained*. He spent an entire spring and summer slamming against our window, as if trying to get in. When I left a nearby door open one morning, he darted in and started slamming himself against the window, trying to get out.

The skills of knowing what makes a difference and how hard to work to bring it about are developed over time on the basis of experimentation. Children sometimes cry in just this spirit, trying to determine what it takes to get a parent to attend. Dating is a string of experiments in learning to deal with sex and togetherness. For some, even choice of livelihood is tentative until confirmed by the results. The limits of individual ability are set, therefore, by the complex interplay of our knowledge of the pressure points of the world, how hard and how long we press, and what strengths and skills we bring to bear.

The Greek commandment, KNOW THYSELF, and its extension demanding that we explore our individual abilities is, therefore, difficult to satisfy. It requires continuing experimental engagement with the world, constant assessment, expansion and retraction of our activities. The surprises of the world and the loose boundaries of our skills to deal with them constitute the great sources of interest, challenge, and satisfaction in our lives. Here, as elsewhere, we know nothing without experience, nothing for sure and nothing that might not change.

OPPORTUNITIES

Talents are worthless without *opportunities* to utilize them. We cannot enjoy activities, no matter how well we might perform them, if the occasion fails to arise or if circumstances do not permit. Sometimes we can create occasions, as we do for celebrating a championship team or for love in the afternoon. But at other times, circumstances turn into mighty masters, constraining our choices or denying us the activities we most desire. We may not have enough food to eat or enough money to visit a dying parent. I may prefer to read the morning paper on the plane, but sickening turbulence interferes. Women seeking an education are, in some cultures, rudely turned away.

Failure of circumstance in the form of lack of facilities, resources, social permission, political freedom, and personal encouragement constitutes a great impediment to human happiness. The fact that many of these factors are necessary even for the development of individual abilities explains why their absence is so devastating. Like plants, people need nurturing soil: without the physical and social necessities, we cannot live or grow.

The success of America is due to its legendary status as a land of opportunity in which all individuals willing to exert themselves can flourish. This image of our land gives strong rhetorical support to the drive for equal opportunity, though not for equal results. Yet opportunity must always be more than the empty possibility of being permitted to do something. In employment, for instance, it must include the enabling condition of education and exclude the limiting condition of the glass ceiling that sets an actual but unacknowledged boundary to promotions.

Some people find it difficult to accept the fact that often opportunities do not present themselves, but must be created. They exist like nested Chinese boxes, where we can look inside the second only after we have opened the first. We must learn to read before we can drive a car, and we must learn to drive before we offer to take trucks coast to coast. Education and acceptable social behavior become, in this way, necessary for virtually all further advancement. The person who fails to take advantage of early, formative opportunities, therefore, forfeits nearly all the good things they make possible.

In Love with Life

Thoughtful parents teach their children that opportunities and failure to take advantage of them are momentous realities. Some things we simply never get a chance to try again. The teenager who hits a bump in the road at high speed, slams his head, and is paralyzed for life cannot drive more slowly next time. Marrying the person one loves, getting treatment for a terrible disease, and trying out for a football team, among many others, are things one can do only at the right time and perhaps only once.

Yet America is not only the land of opportunity but also the home of the second chance. Just as some religions say it is never too late (or too soon) to repent our sins, so Americans think it is always possible to change our ways and start all over again. Even if this view is too optimistic, we can at least switch jobs or fields or professions, and we may find love and meaning late in life. A humane culture devoted to success and the enjoyment of existence encourages people to go back to where they took the wrong turn and lets them try again.

SATISFACTION

Which activities we choose depends not only on what we are good at and on what we have a chance to do, but also on what we have *previously enjoyed*. Since people seek to repeat the pleasurable moments in their lives, past experience serves as a powerful guide to preference. Such guidance is important because the range of activities in which humans can take delight is practically without limit. Curiosity is a natural feature of restless minds; the experimentation to which it leads often discloses unsuspected sources of satisfaction. Moreover, both desires and the plea-sures that come from fulfilling them are contagious: once a few people obtain a pleasure or a possession, no one wants to be left behind.

The cause of happiness is much advanced by the fact that we tend to like what we excel at, and often we excel at what we like. When young people ask me about what they should take as a major in college or choose as a profession in life, I usually tell them to go for whatever they truly like. If their love of a subject or activity is not a momentary infatuation, they are likely to work at it contentedly and to reach a level of relative perfection.

The energy and skill with which we perform our tasks is what such ancient Greek philosophers as Plato and Aristotle called excellence or virtue. The reward of such virtue, they correctly observed, is well-being, which in turn reinforces our desire to be good at what we do. The circular movement of excellence yielding satisfaction that creates a desire for further excellence constitutes one of the great supports of human achievement.

Adults get impatient with young people and insist that they make up their minds about what they want to do with their lives. Such uncertainty, however, is a natural part of growing up in a society that permits choice of lifestyle and profession. Telling children what they ought to like, as we tend to do in raising and educating them, is rarely enough to convince them.

The fact that these suggestions come from adults, who probably have an agenda of their own, makes them suspect at once. So young people delay their decisions, explore, and experiment to see if they can find out for themselves which activities lead to fulfillment. This is a good strategy: since their choices are based on such personal experience, the tastes they acquire tend to be permanent or at least stable.

Unfortunately, however, some people don't take pleasure in the activities where their talents and achievements lie. They may want to be good at what is beyond their reach, hoping for success in medicine or in sports. Or their gifts may qualify them only for boring, dead-end jobs, whose satisfactions are supposed to be below us.

The primary reason for this discrepancy between expectations and reality is the rhetoric of our culture. We are taught to aim high. We are told that anyone can be president, that everyone is a winner, and that we can achieve anything if we want it enough. This makes things difficult for those who don't succeed: they live in gray resentment and see their existence as a stunted reed.

Here again, luckily, the energy of human nature helps us out. If we don't keep stewing over our failures, the bitterness of them soon disappears. Doing *anything* well carries a measure of satisfaction, and if the task presents even a little challenge, we get absorbed in tackling it. Even mindless routine has its rhythms and its quiet tune, so we can relax in the bosom of the familiar.

We are quick to make peace with what there is and to embrace the small compensations of comfort and competence. If we cannot be astronauts or billionaires, there must still be something we can do that's fun. And if we first refuse, and later forget, to think of each activity as a painful compromise, we can sail right on enjoying the small world that is home.

Choosing Activities

SOCIAL STANDARDS

People grow up believing that their ways are not only right but also natural, and that as a result no choice was ever involved in their development. Only upon seeing the variety of human *customs* does the thought of their contingency occur to most of us. Even when they meet general human needs, customs grow out of local circumstance and survive by being freely reproduced from generation to generation. Anything that interferes with these established modes of operation appears to threaten the stability of life.

We must not be surprised, therefore, at seeing that even those who know that their practices enjoy no cosmic prerogatives nevertheless resist changing them. The idea that if we lived by other habits and values than our own, we would not be worse off, and may even do better, enters our heads only to be dismissed. The devil you know is better, most people think, than one who can trick you in novel ways.

Young people and others who see the optionality or staleness of customs make the mistake of thinking that one can transgress them with impunity. Why should one not be able to run around nude, declare oneself a pagan, or dine by biting into a passing cow?

There may be no convincing arguments against such activities, but those who contemplate choosing them are well advised to think of the consequences. An unmarried friend came to be viewed with suspicion by his neighbors because he never put out any garbage. Everyone whose beliefs or actions fall outside the range of tolerable orthodoxy is subject to distrust and retaliation. The visible hand of social disapproval can deal crushing blows against even such minor offenders as people wearing their hair too long or laughing too loud and at the wrong time.

In choosing activities to enjoy, therefore, we must take serious account of the realities of the social world around us. Eccentrics and iconoclasts derive pleasure from violating common expectations, but that luxury is open only to those who are invulnerable or to people who don't care. For the rest, limiting activities to ones that are at least generally acceptable is a wise, if not necessary, strategy.

To some, this may seem an intolerable compromise. But from the standpoint of the individual, social conditions are as much a given as physical limits. Factoring them into our choices makes for a better life, or at least for one less littered with problems.

None of this is to deny that resisting injustice and fighting for an ideal are delightful and worthwhile. Taking the moral high ground gives some people a high: thinking that one is in the right makes for breathless excitement and glowing, sometimes even gloating, satisfaction.

This captures the imagination of a few, and they end up devoting all their energy to denouncing the strong and defending the weak. But such a life is clearly not for the majority. Most of those who have the energy and daring to take a stand swing into action only when and only so long as wickedness touches their lives directly. Many people never resist at all: they subdue unauthorized desires and learn to forget the unfairness and the slights.

The best strategy with social standards may well be to observe them where we must, but to stretch them where we can. All of us have what may be viewed as a line of credit with the community. A few transgressions of custom, especially if they are not outrageous, are permitted, but they reduce the credit stored in the account. Predictability, generous devotion to at least a few members of the community, and thorough conventionality in some facets of life increase the balance.

Whenever we find a socially questionable activity irresistible, therefore, we can draw on our credit. To those who are otherwise stable, much is forgiven. In occasionally refusing to be conventional, we gain the pleasure of doing what we want and contribute to the expansion of what people think decent persons may legitimately do.

VARIETY

Try having your favorite meal for two weeks in a row. How long will it be before you sneak away to grab a hamburger or a club sandwich or anything other than what you feel you have been eating day and night? Uniformity, even if it consists only of the good, repels us. We seek the safe and the certain, yet steady predictability crushes the soul. The invariant lacks excitement, it is always "the same old thing." So we go in search of adventure and embrace change to wake up from the sleep of the ever-same.

Love of *variety* may have a biological basis in our need for sensory stimulation. Alternatively, its origin may reside in the exploratory restlessness of our social life. In either case, it is a powerful reality we must reckon with as we choose actions to enjoy. It penetrates the depths of our consciousness and surfaces in common activities and in unsuspected places.

In eating, for example, few would choose the nutritionally adequate paste designed to feed astronauts. Instead, we want varied tastes, multiple textures, and divergent activities of the mouth to make the meal satisfying. With richly flavored meats, we may choose sour pickles and end with a sweet dessert. We delight in combining things that are smooth, such as mashed potatoes, with harder, resistant meat and with crunchy lettuce and celery. (Without the desire for salt and crunchiness, the potato chip industry would fold.) We also like to alternate easy swallowing with biting and tearing, only to return again and again to the satisfactions of chewing. Our entire repertoire of eating is a study in how to enhance enjoyment through variety.

The same desire for diversity shows itself in human relations. Enjoyment of variance is possible only against a backdrop of stability. Constancy by itself, however, is a quick route to boredom, so old friends have to look for new things to do together in order to sustain their relation. Steadiness without the tease of difference crushes marriages: once caring, sex, and daily interaction become matters of routine, the excitement of living together disappears. Smart couples fight back by continuing to date and by spicing their days with small surprises and delicious spontaneities.

Excessive variety, however, can also wreak havoc with our lives. Some people change jobs so often that they forego advancement. Others move restlessly from state to state and live like lone, rootless nomads. Individuals who like to be "thick" with others use up their friends, while others consume large numbers of sexual partners.

Even when diversity is not great, it can be devastating if it comes at the wrong time. A glance away from the monotony of the road to enjoy the mountains can crash the car. People stuck in poverty tend to be ready dupes for the welcome change promised by get-rich-quick schemes. And even a single fling is enough to ruin a marriage.

Aristotle may well have been right that timing and avoiding too much and too little are central issues in life. Variety is particularly damaging when we have either a surfeit or a desperate shortage of it. Too much denies us the stability we must have, while too little robs us of the excitement of living. To get just what we need, and at the proper time, is a matter of experience and sound judgment. At the very least, it is wise to assess our condition regularly. If everything seems volatile, it is time to send down roots; but if everything is going smoothly, life begs to be shaken up.

Choices

Unfortunately, the skill of making sensible and timely choices cannot be taught by explaining its principles. We can observe people who are good at choosing and try our hands at it to see if we can do as well. Those who are sensitive and smart eventually learn to choose by choosing, and that often means by making mistakes and then not making them again.

This is one of the reasons why children have to be raised to choice: they must be permitted to chart their courses in nearly all matters that do not threaten ruin. Only by choosing and bearing the consequences of their mistakes can they acquire the art of navigating the shallows of a tempting world. The other reason to let people follow their fancy is that the experience of choice reveals the vibrancy of freedom. Without the liberty to embrace what we want, joy nearly always eludes us and, framed in frustration, life loses its allure.

Which activities should we then choose to maximize the enjoyment of life? We must embrace those that our talents and opportunities permit us to undertake, so long as they are satisfying, varied, and not severely at odds with what is socially acceptable. Each of the five considerations we have discussed presents a moving target, changing with time, with alterations in the others, and with the context of our lives.

Abilities expand and then contract with age and depend on opportunities for their development. What we find satisfying also changes as we age and with what others approve or tolerate. Even the need for variety can be vastly reduced by circumstance, as it is in the lives of the severely injured or of the very old, and it varies with what we like.

This suggests that it is impossible to sustain enjoyment of life without being alert and energetic. Continued changes require reflection and timely adjustments, which amount roughly to what the American philosopher John Dewey meant by intelligence. Absent early detection and shrewd response, the contingencies of life can quickly overwhelm us.

On the other hand, it is almost impossible to fail to enjoy life so long as we take it as an adventure that evokes our energetic best. If everything goes wrong, of course, we can suffer defeat and live in misery. But that is rare. For the most part and at least up to a point, the project of intelligence, wringing happiness out of the interplay of our energies with the constraints of the world, is successful. Almost always, life presents at least *something* to be enjoyed.

Changes in the five factors affecting sensible choice and variations in how they interact also suggest considerable individual differences in what makes life good. No one can prescribe what others should enjoy. Often we do not even understand how people can take pleasure in what they do.

Choosing Activities

There are no exceptionless rules in this sphere, only some useful generalizations. We know what many enjoy and we know what is unusual. But no matter how smart, people cannot with assurance predict what others, even what they themselves, will like. No one, moreover, can justly condemn what is sincerely enjoyed, so long as it doesn't interfere with the lives and enjoyments of others.

That different persons may wisely choose varied activities does not mean that values are relative. On the contrary, they are firmly grounded in the sorts of people we are and in our circumstances. Since mere hope or belief renders nothing excellent, we can be wrong, very wrong, about what is good for us. In choosing things to do and to enjoy, we must deal with realities: our talents, our opportunities, and what we can delight in set objective limits to our world.

But genuine differences among individuals make it unreasonable to demand that everyone act the same way and value the same things. The resulting variety disturbs only people who seek a uniformity that produces replicas of them everywhere. Free choice leading to individual differences makes for a richer moral order than enforced regularity.

An emphasis on enjoying the activities of life does not imply that pleasure is the only thing worthwhile. On the contrary, aiming for gratification is usually a mistake. The very idea that pleasures are *had* suggests that a passive and possessive rather than an active and open attitude is appropriate to their pursuit. Pleasures are feelings that attend stimulation, not living enjoyments of participation in the movement of things. The active side of life offers itself continually to be savored; when we accept its invitation, we delight in the process, not in stimulation and its result.

5

Distorted Activities

Leaving Others Alone

Few things attract people as much as telling others what to do. Telling is not commanding; happily, the modern world has reduced opportunities to order people about. Commanding, moreover, involves not only rights but obligations as well. To give orders is to wrench the decisions of others away from them and thereby to acquire responsibility for the outcomes. Kibitzing with people is less risky and more satisfying than taking over their lives. One can set forth to them, in detail and repeatedly, what they should do, and then enjoy the gloating satisfaction of shaking or pointing fingers if they didn't listen.

Vast growth in the number of consultants suggests not only how many people are prepared to offer advice but also how many are willing to pay for it. Teachers, financial planners, stewardesses, auto mechanics, psychologists, fitness trainers, dieticians, interior decorators, doctors, waiters, travel agents, neighbors, parents, and distant acquaintances all take delight in telling us what to do. They claim more refined sensitivity, better taste, keener insight, and greater knowledge than presumably we can muster. Any person ready to act on the recommendations of others must be busy day and night.

Instructions on what to do with our lives change from harmless nuisance to threatening interference when people present them in the language of morality. Matters as mundane or indifferent as what we do in our spare time and how we use our money are then recast in terms of right and wrong, entitling strangers to demand that we comply with the requirements of justice or duty. Those who fail to heed these calls can be denounced as morally insensitive and perhaps even wicked, and the power of the community can be employed to bring them in line.

In this way, what might well be left to the diversity of individual choice is made uniform and compulsory. We set and enforce social standards concerning how people can look and behave, and what they must say and believe. Women, for example, are expected to enhance their appearance by the use of make-up, but many people feel repelled at the sight of men wearing lipstick and eyeliner. Hair must not be too long or unkempt, demeanor must be dignified or serious or at least not rambunctious, and everyone ought to hold a job instead of living off fish in the sea and berries in the woods. What we say must fit the conventions of the day; grave consequences befall those whose words offend or who address others in the wrong way.

It never seems to occur to us to ask what difference it makes if people violate the rules of etiquette or of such arm-twisting ethics. What if some persons smell or wear no socks when it snows or won't speak to anyone or sit for a week at the bus stop on a bench? Such behaviors have natural consequences: people will want to have nothing to do with individuals who engage in them. We don't need to reinforce or justify our desire to avoid such persons by calling what they do wrong and pronouncing them sick or depraved. We can simply leave them alone, which is to let them seek their own good in their own way, so long as they honor us with the same respectful distance.

Letting people make their own decisions is a great, though little-practiced, virtue. We deny this right even to those we love, spending endless energy running the lives of our spouses and children. When we refrain from telling them what to do, we demand that they tell us what they did, as if they had to justify themselves. Functionaries in our institutions spend their time devising rules to order the behavior of customers and employees, and whenever frustrated people sigh, "There ought to be a law," some legislators are ready to pass it.

Our efforts to set people right and to make the world operate correctly keep us too busy to remember the value of freedom. Yet choice is vital for happiness; what others impose on us is rarely enjoyed. Since being free is being free to fail, we pay the price of liberty in mistakes. That is why it makes sense to think of life as a glorious series of trials and errors, of experiments that match our wits against the constraining might of the world. It does little good to tell people what they want to try out and how. As the great champion of freedom John Stuart Mill observed, the knowledge others have of what's good for us cannot rival our personal assessment.

Distorted Activities

We find it difficult to believe that some things we are used to and have come to expect don't really make a lot of difference to most of us. Whether women walk around in skirts or in pants, whether our neighbors prefer homosexual or heterosexual relations, whether people hold their jobs for life or change them once a year, and whether we have two presidential candidates to vote for or three or half a dozen matter relatively little in the larger scheme of things. A few individuals may have vested interests in preserving established customs, but most people remain untouched by the vast majority of issues that cause moral outrage and social controversy.

This does not justify our failing to take an interest in the life of our communities. To the contrary, drawing a clear line between changeable matters of custom and concerns of deeper moral significance enhances our commitment to righting genuine wrongs. Those who hark back to how things used to be express not their love of the good but their discomfort with change. The world does not have to be just so; we need to let it bear all manner of fruit and enjoy its transformations.

Impulse and Control

We think many things people do are strange, unacceptable, or immoral, yet these activities only *seem* distorted. They may be expressions of personal peculiarities or harmlessly unconventional ways of defining the self. If we could see the world from the perspective of the objectionable persons, the oddity would disappear and everything they do would look natural and right.

Nevertheless, some human activities really are distorted and don't merely seem so. Some fail to serve the purposes of the individual; others harm the nurturing community. Certain actions fall short on both counts. We punish people, for example, to deny them the benefits gained through criminal acts. Actions that harm others come around, in this way, to hurt the perpetrator as well.

The most frequent reason why our efforts don't contribute to our happiness is lack of clarity about what we want. Since learning what satisfies is an arduous journey leading through desert and swamp, the confusion is understandable and difficult to avoid. So many things capture the attention and evoke the desires of the young that we can hardly expect them to know how to separate what is of real value from the shine of empty promises.

Though pain and disappointment teach us distrust of what looks good, of what we call "too good to be true," the lesson must be relearned at every turn. Appearances continue deceiving because they are so attractive that we cannot believe they could hurt. Some persons never quit falling in love with the wrong people or falling for get-rich-quick schemes. Others keep smoking and drinking, crazily convinced that what feels good now can never be the source of harm.

The intricate balance between instant delight and long-term flourishing presents humans with an endless string of problems, which means boundless opportunities for distorted or harmful acts. Economists and grocery store ads depict consumers as walking computers who make accurate calculations of their needs and the amount to spend to meet them. In reality, people who go shopping for food when hungry buy more than they would otherwise; the desire of the moment overwhelms good judgment. When the harm that flows from our actions is delayed, as in smoking, we find it easy to throw caution to the wind. And we allow long-term planning to be violently abused: it gets mugged in procrastination, mauled by inadequate care of our bodies, and massacred in love. Impulse does not rule human life but raids it to spoil the harvest.

The dean of a famous university divided his days into exquisitely planned fifteen-minute segments. Everything ran like clockwork until his wife started complaining that they never did anything on the spur of the moment. So he had his secretary arrange a spontaneous getaway for the two of them for the following spring. Such people, lacking impulsiveness, strike us as dead on the inside, or at least boring. They seem to have no life in them and no time for play and fun.

Yet people who are constantly spontaneous wear us out. They search for the interesting and try to be interesting themselves. They wish to surprise us by what they say and do, and to be surprising they must be unpredictable. The few individuals like this I have known have always made me yearn for stability and dull peace. Focused on the moment, they invariably get in trouble: they drink and eat too much, hate regular jobs, and repeatedly run short of money.

How to combine spontaneity with due concern for the future is simply the question of how to live well or without regrets. A good life has to be reasonably long, and paying for the impulsiveness of youth with early death or lingering disease casts a pall on the entire experience. So we need to find ways to control most of our impulses and to convert the rest into wholesome spontaneity. The power of passion, its promise of instant release, makes the task very difficult. Hope for accomplishing it rests in the hands of habit and imagination.

The grip of heedless acts is easiest to break in early childhood. Those who are taught caution in their dealings with the world tend to avoid costly mistakes. Children rewarded for exploring the distant outcomes of what they do grow up with a measure of foresight and control. Without such upbringing, people have to rely on the power of mind, a weaker though not negligible force. When properly motivated, for instance by fear, the imagination can envision the future with a vividness that compels action. A friend stopped smoking after he visited his uncle dying of lung cancer. He later told me that, in his mind's eye, he saw himself in the hospital bed wheezing and coughing blood.

We may think that the best way to gain knowledge of what we need and want is by learning who we are. Older people like to make fun of recent college graduates who wish to take a year or two to "find" themselves. A little time away to prepare for the pressures of marriage and career is not a bad thing, and it is especially good because the young can enjoy themselves with abandon. Why, after all, should free time be reserved for the retired, many of whom are too tired or too sick to get the most out of it? But, useful as distancing reflection may be, it can never bring the desired result if we want to discover the hidden core of our being, the precious meat inside the walnut shell of privacy.

The self shares the fate of everything in the turning world. It goes through revolutions of growth and decay; its structure and complexion change and cannot give us guidance once and for all. Worse, those who look to our nature to tell us what we need and want have it backward. Noting what satisfies is the only approach we have to our inner character. We find out who we are through ceaseless experiments in living, through struggling to learn what fulfills us or permits us rest. And even these goals change with time, so seeking the good out of season leads to damaging, distorted activities.

Here, again, the way in which necessity and joy fuse helps us out. We have no alternative to the search for piecemeal fulfillment, to the lifelong pursuit of goals that may or may not satisfy. But this activity is also the glorious adventure of shaping and reshaping ourselves into the sort of people we truly want to be. Our selves are like the houses we inhabit: we repair and expand them, renovate and redecorate them, with exquisite care and doting pleasure.

Self-Destruction

Much as people tend to love their homes, some surprise us by burning them down. Some also destroy themselves, for reasons we can't always fathom. Human activities sometimes become so distorted that they poison the soil that grows them, impeding the processes of life or dissolving them altogether. Suicide is the best-known instance of such fury against the source, but it is not the most puzzling. Slower and more subtle ways of sabotaging life abound and raise questions about their motivation.

A few people kill themselves as an expression of weariness with life, but many more as a result of temporary distress or of a deeper and persistent misery. Not all of these are distorted activities because, for persons terminally ill and suffering constant pain, for example, suicide may be an appropriate course of action. Revulsion at such self-destruction is natural, but not for that reason right. The vehemence of the condemnation reveals no sympathy for the suffering, only the anger of our threatened love of life.

Many among us dull themselves to life, perhaps unable to deal with the keen edge of its challenge. They permit small problems to immobilize them to the point where they have to take medicines to face the day. Or they try to escape conflict or disappointment through the nirvana of alcohol and drugs. Cushioning or avoiding contact with reality is a terrible loss: people who cannot live by tackling facts directly never live. They see the movement of things as in a distant mirror and enter the water in a diver's bell.

Even so, taking pills to cope or drugs to brighten the day is not always a deviant or damaging activity. Some depressed people, though I suspect far fewer than we think, genuinely cannot operate without medication; a bit of Prozac lifts their spirits and restores their joy in life. And drugs and alcohol can be used to enhance existence, not only to destroy it. A drink or two at a party or the occasional chemical to open the doors of perception can enrich our embrace of the world. The key, as Humpty-Dumpty said, remains who is to be in charge. We lose control if we turn to drugs for help and if we ever feel we *need* another drink.

Cases of self-mutilation, on the other hand, are almost without exception distorted activities. When Van Gogh cut off his ear, he accomplished nothing good. The situation is no different when people who suffer from bipolar disease inflict wounds on themselves, or when psychopaths vent their fury on their own bodies. Such individuals may not know what they do, or they may be unable to stop themselves. In either case, their actions are lamentable events past voluntary control, requiring loving care or treatment by the community.

The subtlety of some forms of self-sabotage puts them beyond the reach of diagnosis and care. Inexplicably, some people do not permit themselves to succeed. As the common saying goes, they "snatch defeat from the jaws of victory." They undo themselves not by negligence or lack of effort, but through positive, though perhaps unintended, missteps. Just when the contract is to be signed, they surprise everyone by saying something that raises doubts in the buyer's mind. They embarrass themselves by uncharacteristically crude behavior when a kind comment or two would bring them great benefits. They stumble when they lead in the race for which they have prepared for years.

What can account for such behavior? Persons who sabotage themselves are not buffoons who get laughs and attention for goofing up. They are by no means incompetent, and to all appearances they mean to flourish. If talented human beings vigorously pursuing reasonable goals normally succeed, there is no reason for such people to fail. Yet they do, placing obstacles in their own way and denying themselves the joys of accomplishment.

We are far from having discovered the secret complexities of the human self. Twisted growths and thorny involutions luxuriate below the level of consciousness, in the depths of the soul. Self-saboteurs may quietly believe they are wicked or at least unworthy of victory in the affairs of life. Or they may be so convinced of their incompetence that they squash all evidence to the contrary. They may also be angry at themselves and, adopting the attitude of their parents, punish themselves simply for existing. Whatever their motivation, their course through life is sad in the extreme. Instead of enjoying the flow of energy and its orchard of rewards, they shackle themselves to their tangled values and turn existence into living hell.

Nastiness

Despite persistent complaints about its dangers, modern life is astonishingly safe and stable. Measured against the days when highwaymen made travel deadly, or even against the crime and corruption of nineteenth century London, our existence displays unparalleled peace and security. Compared to subsisting in nature, as do birds and chipmunks even in the yard, our lives show a measure of protection and control unimaginable to animals.

Only our security can explain our stunned dismay at the occasional moments of violence we encounter. If we kept nature in mind, swift and horrible death would not surprise us. I recently saw a hawk on a busy campus swoop down on a pigeon, catch it and, tearing the flesh from its writhing body, devour it. And though I live within city limits, one day in the winter a fox arrived and within seconds captured and carried away a squirrel. Our relation to living, and to dying, would be radically different if we had to confront contingencies like these every hour.

Fortunately we don't. But every benefit has a price. The orderly and secure ways of civilized existence make us feel that life goes on indefinitely, that death is an extraordinary or irregular event. Moreover, having grown up trusting others, we come to believe that cheating, lying, and wickedness are unusual aberrations. Crooks think of such convictions as naive and celebrate them as the foundation of their success. Kind and honest people are easy to exploit; the newspapers are full of stories of the ruthless fleecing the unsuspecting.

Decent people find it difficult to believe that not everyone is sensible and fair. Without experience of human depravity and without much knowledge of history, they simply cannot imagine the horrors of Bosnia, Cambodia, sundry African nations, and the Holocaust. Yet it is crucial to remember that some human beings have learned to be evil and that, under layers of socialization, even civilized persons have a dark and nasty side.

The level of human destructiveness ranges from barbed tongue to barbarous massacre. In some cases, even a snide comment can inflict stinging hurt. A distinguished British professor once told me he hated "nice Americans." He was convinced remarks that drew no blood were not worth making. Such attitudes can build or sustain an entire culture of verbal mischief and mayhem.

Individuals raised with beliefs of this sort labor under the mistaken assumption that it takes more effort to be kind and helpful to people than to obstruct their passage. To smile is, in fact, no more difficult than to parade around with frown and bite, ready to punish everyone for wrongs they did not commit. It is better by far to be a friend to the world and, even if helping its work is not always easy or possible, to cheer it on from a distance, delighting in its success.

In Love with Life

For thousands of years, children have been taught that their happiness and the good fortune of others in their communities are inseparably fused. Our dependence on each other is so great that this is largely true. Yet there are free-riders who profit from social life without making a contribution and people who lift themselves by crushing everyone in their way. The human race has not yet developed enough wisdom to eliminate the incentives for such behavior or to annul its benefits. As a result, some people continue to engage in distorted activities harmful to others because they find it in their interest to do so.

Among these anti-social persons, those bent on pursuing their own happiness tend to be less dangerous than individuals who take pleasure in the failure of their rivals. Cultivation of selfish goals can involve brushing the concerns of others aside. But, sad as that is, it implies only indifference to alien goods, not positive ill will. Egoists don't understand that the human world is committed to having people flourish by helping others do the same, so they hardly notice claims that are not their own. Wicked persons, by contrast, target their fellows for pain; they are prepared, as the British philosopher Bertrand Russell once said, to lose an eye so long as their enemies lose two.

And for such people, every person is an enemy. They act as if happiness were a competitive good, so that if others get any, less is left for them. This is a disastrous misunderstanding of human nature. Happiness, like laughter, creates more of itself; by killing it in others, we eliminate a grand source of our own satisfaction. This is why wicked people have a sour disposition. The song of birds, the kiss of lovers, the cry of victory all embitter them. Life enjoying life burns like a fire all around them and they lack the water to put out the flames.

If they can't destroy these happy people, at least they wish them dead. Desiring the death of others is a widespread distorted activity, though one that does more harm to those engaging in it than to the people whose ill fortune they seek. Some wish loved ones dead because obligations to them have become a burden. A man who had divorced his wife once told me that he hoped her new husband would die, so he could get her back. Wealthy parents who give little to their children while alive are inviting their offspring to think of inheritance and to long for their demise. This yearning is one of very few activities utterly without value: fortunately, it does not by itself contribute to the death of anyone, yet it breeds guilt whether it is fulfilled or not.

Some have claimed that wickedness is a natural outcome of competition in the world. Setting humans against each other, they say, causes them to wish their rivals ill. This sounds plausible but is in fact quite wrong. If rivalry were a struggle for existence, we would kill without a second thought. But the human world is different from nature: for us, competing is a way of life, not of death.

Sports teams matching strength and skill against each other are not bent on destruction. On the contrary, the rivalry would be over if one of the teams were wiped out. The point is to prevail while playing by the rules, and the rules safeguard the future of both sides. If we look below the level of competition, therefore, we see pervasive cooperation: the concern for winning presupposes a greater shared interest in continued rivalry. The league, expressing this common interest, wants every team as strong as it can be. Since winning against weak competition is insignificant, the weal of all teams is a vital concern of each.

Horrors

Primitive persons don't realize that the human world is built, in this way, to sustain and celebrate life. This is a vast communal undertaking that involves, in the end, the entire human race. Its motto was articulated by the wonderfully democratic utilitarian philosophers of nineteenth century England as "Each is to count for one and no one for more than one." We can flourish only together and only if we commit to settling our disagreements by words.

Those who don't understand the differences between brutal nature and humane society try to advance their cause by force of arms. People who swing at others or shoot them are throwbacks to an earlier age, black holes in the bright sky of civilized life. We have reason to hope that the level of organized violence in the world will continue to decline and that spontaneous personal assaults—beatings and murders and rapes—will become sad curiosities in the next few hundred years.

For now, unfortunately, many persons still take pleasure in hurting others and in frustrating, even destroying, their lives. The war they wage on their fellows is not always illegal; the law bans only unsubtle cruelties. Children can be beaten and otherwise abused, employees can be humiliated and the elderly can be reduced to penury. Even when laws are violated, enforcement can be lax and punishment distant and unsure.

Distorted Activities

In this respect, civilized nations suffer from a failure of nerve. As a result of unwillingness to leave others alone, they have crammed the criminal law full of absurd prohibitions. We are permitted to kill ourselves by smoking tobacco but not to have a pleasant evening smoking pot. Certain forms of consensual sex are banned, and masturbation is still illegal in some states. Riding without a seatbelt and making moonshine are banned with the same vigor as mass murder. Silly rules are silly to enforce, and the seriousness and the majesty of the criminal code are compromised when we can't stomach insisting that all of it be obeyed.

Enforcement of the grab bag of rules we have created is further jeopardized by a false humanitarian concern. Many among us feel that executing people for any crime, even depriving them of their liberty, is morally problematic. At least partly as a result, punishments do not follow swiftly and firmly upon the crime, confirming offenders in their belief that breaking the law is not a losing gamble.

Those who take joy in life don't want to take the lives of others. Yet we cannot permit individuals to delight in distorted activities that threaten the existence and security of innocent people. Lacking knowledge of how to reform hardened mass murderers, what are we to do to keep them at bay? The question of what is humane must be asked in the context of what will do the job. And the job is not just to keep this person from doing this again, but to make sure everyone knows the consequences of such acts.

In the end, therefore, it comes down to a sort of public education. We must convince people who find severely distorted activities attractive that it is more painful to engage in them than to exert self-control. Clearly drawn lines and quick, severe, yet fair punishments for transgressing them help to make this point. The message to convey is that in humane societies people are free to do much or all that relates to them alone, but not to hurt or murder others. To hold people responsible is to teach them responsibility. We must trust people to be able to learn; almost invariably, they will start acting properly once the costs of not doing so are clear.

The same approach may slowly reduce the desire of terrorists and warlike states to create conflagrations around the globe. No person and no state should want to run the lives of others. So we need to say clearly that we respect independence and wish to leave everyone alone, but we will not tolerate aggressive and destructive acts. This should give ample general guidance to all concerning what they must not do. The horrors of human history will not likely be repeated if people of good will resolve to stop the madness as soon as it starts.

6

Tiredness with Life

Enough

Janet's husband worked himself to death. He left her a rich widow when she was barely fifty. For the next twenty-five years, she lived quietly but well. She never remarried, but she was a loyal friend to many, making sure that everyone around her shared in her good fortune. She lived in New York in an apartment overlooking Central Park, bought herself everything she wanted and traveled all over the globe.

Age brought Janet no illness but, when she reached seventy-five, she confided to a few close friends that she had had enough. She thought she had seen and done everything of interest to her, and there was no point in repeating things. She felt tired of life and tired of the world, and no new activity her friends suggested could get her excited.

Janet quietly gave away most of her valuables and, a few months later, attempted suicide. To her great distress, the sleeping pills she had been hoarding were not enough to kill her. Discovered by a neighbor, she landed in a hospital where they pumped her stomach and sent her, in accordance with New York law, to see a psychiatrist. The indignity of the forced medicalization of her private, intimate relation to life angered her and cemented her resolve. In less than a year, she attempted suicide again and died, her note to friends assured them, happily and at peace.

Looked at from the outside, Janet's decision to die is difficult to understand. When I tell her tale, people usually begin, "If I had her money . . ." Our love of life renders her story baffling; why would someone in reasonably good health, with lots of friends and plenty of money not be able to think of a thousand things to do? *We* can find no answer to such questions as Why not see Hong Kong again? And if not Hong Kong, then Rome or Hawaii. *We* are ready to pack our bags; why should she not have been interested?

Those who take the highway of imagination, however, may be able to behold the world through eyes similar to hers. She knew she hadn't seen everything—no one has. But she had no interest in seeing the rest, and no interest means no energy. Sometimes, the energy simply runs out and doing anything becomes a chore. Then people feel there is nothing to live for, that no aim deserves the struggle to attain it. They hunker down and wait quietly for the moment of release or else take matters into their own hands and kill themselves. That may have been what happened to Janet.

The silent emptiness that leads to the wish to die is different from the internal shambles left upon the collapse of major projects. People who have built their lives around a grand scheme that fails can find themselves in desperate straits. A student of mine so wanted to go to medical school that he spent every waking hour thinking about it. He volunteered in the emergency room and offered himself as a subject for experiments. To compensate for his weak academic record, he took two years after college to study more science. When even that did not gain him admission, he enrolled in a Third World medical school, hoping to transfer later to a better institution. The final failure of his dreams left him cynical and bitter, doing everything he could to make the world pay for his disappointment.

This man was internally destroyed, but he never tired of life. His energy remained untouched; he simply refocused it on the unrelenting pursuit of nastiness. Others who face disappointments in love or in their line of work may be despondent for a while and, at the low point of their depression, take their lives. But their acts show no lessening of drive, only frustration, confusion, or temporary lack of aim. The same is true of young people who, in a moment of haste, decide to kill themselves. Their energy swirls like a hurricane and, without adequate guidance, devours itself. They are not tired of life, only at a loss for what to do with it.

Janet's situation was different from any of these. She had simply had enough. Most people who feel that way are racked by chronic pain or suffer from a terminal disease. Their cases are not difficult to understand: combating pain uses up all their energy and having no prospects renders life meaningless. But Janet's condition was different from theirs also. She was perfectly well, and life presented neither problem nor struggle. She had just lived long enough and now wanted rest.

Such exhaustion has, on occasion, taken the form of a contagious social phenomenon. The end of the nineteenth century witnessed, especially among intellectuals, an astonishing level of weariness with life. This was the first time in the history of humankind that boredom became a serious topic for reflection and literary effort. Algernon Charles Swinburne, a British poet of the day, may have offered the darkest of distorted visions in writing,

> From too much love of living,
>   From hope and fear set free,
> We thank with brief thanksgiving
>   Whatever gods may be
> That no life lives for ever;
> That dead men rise up never;
> That even the weariest river
>   Winds somewhere safe to sea.

Tiredness like this leads to rejection of life, of our deepest hopes, of everything beautiful and vibrant. By a horrible inversion, only death seems beautiful and only rest worth having, though even they must not be pursued aggressively. Patient waiting will get us what we have always wanted: not to be. Until the passivity of life gives way to a greater passivity, we have to suffer boredom with a heavy sigh.

Challenges

Weariness with everything we naturally value may be viewed as the response of well-to-do people to an easy life.

Tiredness with Life

Janet clearly experienced the decline in energy that comes with aging. But she probably also found life less challenging than is necessary for full enjoyment. She thought she had seen enough; had she wanted to do anything, go anywhere, or buy the corner store, she could simply have written a check. Would she have felt the same way about life if her trip to Hong Kong had been the experience of a lifetime, achieved by years of planning and penny-pinching self-denial?

Many people find life excruciatingly hard. Circumstance or misfortune makes them struggle for everything they get. Worry and sorrow cloud their days; frustration is their walking-companion. Some stumble along, barely avoiding ruin. Astonishingly, such people seem not to run out of energy. They grit their teeth and get the most they can out of life. Never having got enough of anything they wanted, it would never occur to them to throw in the towel and say that they're finished.

More fortunate individuals, on the other hand, can afford the luxury of being weary of life. Since they don't have to toil incessantly, they have time to be bored. Without compulsory activities, without the labor the world exacts for sustaining life, choice of what to do becomes difficult. If imagination is lacking, they may come to think that no challenge is worthy of their efforts. The general paralysis that follows drives joy out of life and puts tedium in its place. Those who don't get tired by evening get tired of life.

Winning the lottery can destroy an undisciplined person. A similar experience was reported to me by an accountant who helped his employer, an aging investor, get rich. When the old man married a young woman, she insisted on cleaning house by sweeping out her husband's former circle of friends and employees. My friend was given a large sum for his services and sent away. He came to me distraught, complaining that life seemed empty, with no challenge left. He had always wanted to be rich and now that he suddenly reached his goal, he had no other objectives to put in its place. "How do I find a new challenge?" he kept asking over dinner, as if he thought I could give him some of mine.

Parents who work hard to provide everything for their children complain that often the result is distressing. Young people quickly learn to take good life in our affluent society for granted and to think they don't have to do anything to deserve or to sustain it. The parents fear that if such attitudes become cemented into habits, their offspring will never know the value of money and may grow into indolent, irresponsible adults. Little work and no appreciation of the need for it can, in their view, lead only to the boredom of a meaningless existence.

Though understandable, this concern of generous parents is, luckily, without foundation. Their offspring tend to be anything but lazy, pursuing their own projects with an abandon that annoys their elders. These activities, to be sure, bring pleasure and not profit of the sort parents see as useful for later life. But should we expect young people to be stupid and not take advantage of the chance to enjoy their youth? Removing parental support permits the economic system to work its wonders; soon, it yokes the young to the service of others as the price of meeting their needs.

The sense of meaninglessness that attends sudden wealth and the easy life is a powerful reminder of the importance of challenges. Problems energize us and when energy flows freely, life is delicious. Challenges focus the mind and mobilize our resources; they invite us to exercise our powers. They force us to come up with new ideas and to see which of them will work. This is what it means to experiment, and when we turn life into a string of intelligent experiments, our excitement about the results spreads to the process of achieving them. In this way, every day allows us to enjoy the delightful tests of inventiveness that scientists experience in their labs.

People faced with an ample collection of challenges do not grow tired of their lives. Some of our aims must be satisfiable within a short time, others only in the somewhat distant future. A fiercely well-organized high school teacher of mine once said that she kept daily notes of what she had to do. She made sure, she explained, that each list contained some items that could be done at once and some that could not be finished and would have to be advanced from day to day. I thought this was proof of her pedantic ways, missing the deep wisdom of her practice.

Whether we like it or not, a great deal of what we do is routine. To concede, therefore, that the commonplace and the necessary can yield no satisfaction is to give up on far too much of life. We can see our daily chores as obstacles to enjoyment or as rich sources of it. Even changing a light bulb or running the vacuum can give a measure of satisfaction as it is marked off the list. And the pleasure increases if we do it well, but especially if we accomplish it in a different or innovative way.

We must not expect too much; small activities give small satisfactions. If we focus on the rewards, we will never confuse doing the laundry with a night of love. But for all that, even running the washing machine offers some compensations, not the least of which is the welcome knowledge that we are preparing for more interesting things. So in performing our necessary routines, we can feel that we make headway in sustaining a good life or in creating a better one.

The satisfying feature of small challenges is that they can be met; we can dispose of them quickly and completely. Paradoxically perhaps, the intrigue of a more significant challenge is that we cannot finish work on it for a while. The continuity of effort it requires gives definition and continuity to the self. We are what we want, at least in the sense that our larger projects shape our lives and characters.

This is so not only in novels that trace the effects of love and other grand passions on human life. It holds true also of the people we meet at the grocery store and see driving down the street. Our jobs, the personal and social responsibilities we shoulder, even our hobbies and avocations exercise a profound influence over our careers as human beings. Our plans and our tasks, what we mean to achieve and who we want to become make us the persons we are. Projects are hooks the future sinks in us to draw us to itself.

The American philosopher Josiah Royce called the larger challenges that wed us to the future "loyalties," that is, commitments to a project or a cause. Such loyalties, consisting of the wholehearted pursuit of purposes, create excitement and energy. They involve investing our efforts in things beyond the narrow confines of the isolated person. We can be ourselves only by growing into new or larger selves, that is, by expanding the scope of our interests and activities in both space and time. Given the differences among humans, the causes we embrace are naturally varied. But they need not be grand or governed by ideology; they can be personal and even quirky. So long as they are non-destructive, devotion to them matters more than their content or nature.

We seem to do best when challenges come in a variety of sizes, from feeding the dog to choosing and executing a plan of life. A rich mix of them never leaves us without the satisfaction of knowing that we have done something and the urge to get on and do a lot more. Without both of these, life freezes in us and, like planes that stall or mountain climbers who stop to look down, we lose momentum and begin to fall.

Wimps

Most people get fatigued by nightfall or at some point before they go to bed. This is not tiredness with life, only the natural depletion of energy by the activities of the day. The next morning they are full of life again, ready to tackle whatever may come their way. The attitude with which we arise sets the tone for the entire day. At a low point in his life, a friend of mine decided that he would never again crawl out of bed. He started leaping out, with the resolve of one who plunges into cold water after an hour in the sun. The surge of energy his morning jump-start released carried through for hours and came to symbolize his determination to take on the whole world.

In Love with Life

Some persons get up in slow motion, trailing low moans. They are not tired of life but afraid of it. They believe their exertions will be futile and they will suffer defeat. A small voice in the middle of their heads keeps repeating that the odds are against them in everything they try. Even when they have no evidence of failure, never having tried such things before, they are convinced they cannot succeed; the novelty of some acts is enough to scare them off.

This wet-mop mentality exerts a crushing effect on life. I once found a student suffering from it and could hardly understand how he made it out of high school and into college. The pained look on his face and his gestures of resignation come vividly to mind even after many years. When we talked, he reminded me of a mop soaked in water; he would go limp each time I tried to make him stand up and face a problem. He could not take the exam because he hadn't studied; studying would, in any case, do no good because of the complexity of the material; his classmates wouldn't want to help him overcome this difficulty; and even if they did, they are not likely to be near their phones or to answer them.

The only response one could make to such systematic defeatism was the angry, "Alright, then, don't do anything." This was exactly what he wanted to hear, though he knew he shouldn't like it. So he would move slowly down a list of complaints, wailing in words, without a tear or change of voice. If he was tired of anything, it was of his own misfortune or impotence, not life. Yet he never understood the extent to which his misery was of his own devising.

People with such systematic aversion to doing anything are, fortunately, rare. But many are tired of one or another facet of their lives and somehow can't find the strength to do much about it. Marriage is a tiresome dead-end relation for more couples than admit it. Boring jobs and dull personal relations color existence gray for a large number of individuals. Others find themselves exhausted by worries about money, children, or the uncertainty of their future. Many feel drained by stress or overwhelmed by endless demands on their time.

None of this is surprising in the least. The difficulty comes in understanding why certain people can summon the energy to change their situation while others, immobilized, drown in their sea of grief. External circumstances go only part of the way toward explaining the inextinguishable life in some. We know that the habit, acquired in childhood, of attacking problems with energy is an important factor. Repeated success solidifies this tendency until vigorous assault upon whatever ails us becomes the natural response. We also know that energy is contagious, so that individuals surrounded by people ready to get things done tend to tackle problems optimistically themselves.

But things don't always work out that way. Unaccountably, people who have seen little but defeat rally and find ways to deal with whatever stands in their way. For reasons equally difficult to see, persons with the best habits get derailed and lose the vigor that energized their success. The rise of energy is a daily, ordinary mystery that resists explanation as much as where the next word comes from when we speak or write. All of a sudden, it's just there, welling up from the depths of the soul as an expression of its love for life. The sadness of wimps is that their souls are wilted; they can't muster the courage to love life with abandon.

Loss and Guilt

Another sort of tiredness descends on some who suffer great personal loss. People whose beloved spouses or children die tend to lose their appetite for life. Their problem is not that they have done it all or that there is something they lack the strength to handle. Departure of the people they love the most leaves them forlorn, and doing anything at all seems pointless and empty.

Anyone who has suffered great loss can understand the grief that leaves us enfeebled and unable to cope. Food ceases to taste right, and we feel as if the last ounce of energy has drained from our limbs. Everything once fun loses its attraction until, in the end, even getting dressed and preparing dinner become unbearable burdens. Life turns, in this way, into a listless waiting for something to happen, a quiet impatience for death.

The exhaustion is so great that, though people think they want to die, they cannot find the energy to kill themselves. Just as well; as time heals the wound, the natural drives return and life begins to feel sweet once again. Suicide is best viewed as something that we can always or nearly always do, so there is no point in doing it now. Life must be not only horrible, but also without hope of improvement before it makes sense to give terminating it a moment's thought. Our love of life is so powerful that it finds a way to add flashes of enjoyment even to a sad and limited existence. To escape the pain forever is to forego the joy—a sacrifice too many make too soon.

Sometimes the tiredness and the wish to die derive from a sense of guilt. Humans suffer from an unstable mix of opinions: they think the world of themselves but also believe they are unworthy and flawed. The first of these views begets arrogance, the second guilt. We may feel guilty because we think it is wrong for better people to have perished and for us to live on. Or we may feel responsible for not having done everything we could for our loved ones while they were still alive. The guilt saps our energy and lays waste to joy in life; even when our normal tendency to take delight in what we do breaks through, we are tormented by the dreadful thought that we have no right to have a good time.

Guilt over what we have failed to do for loved ones can be prevented with ease, though sometimes at a relatively high cost. We can undertake to do everything in our power to help them lead better lives. This is loving them while the love still counts, while caring makes a difference. It may involve sacrifices and it requires self-control. But the hallmark of civilized people is that they can curb their immediate urges by thinking of what the future will bring; hence, they put up with current unpleasantness to secure later peace of mind.

We can reinforce this tendency to give by believing that God keeps track of what we do. We can make it a habit by the resolve to act out of love, as Christianity and other religions command. Or we may think that loss through death or emotional separation is final and that, therefore, opportunities for caring and reconciliation may never come again. In any case, those who do everything they can for the people they love, and for people in need, feel no guilt upon their passing.

Unfortunately, actions cannot rid us of the generalized form of guilt. Some people experience that as a result of their good fortune in flourishing or in having at least survived, while others feel that however much they do for others, it is never enough. These are issues not of right or wrong behavior, but of sensible or silly beliefs. Since what people think is more difficult to change than what they do, relieving such guilt faces mighty obstacles.

Nevertheless, it may help to remind ourselves that we cannot be held responsible for our luck. Good fortune measures the difference between our efforts and our achievements, between how much we do and how much more we get. We neither earn nor deserve it, so there is no reason to be concerned about our unworthiness. It is more blessed to give than to receive, but we must also learn to accept gifts gratefully and without protest.

Further, we might find it helpful to identify the false assumption behind the charge that we never do enough. For people like ourselves, limited in every conceivable way, trying hard and doing what we can should suffice. Although sometimes we can do more than we thought, we can't keep on doing more and more. We shouldn't, therefore, have to feel guilty for failing to feed everyone in New Delhi or to defeat alcoholism among the Eskimo. Those who think we should, smuggle infinity into our souls, with all the romantic unhappiness that involves. Such grandeur crushes our modest dignity, and we end as fools shouldering responsibility for what we did not cause and could never undo.

Caring

The best way to combat tiredness with life is by staying alert and oriented and taking an interest in everything that goes on. Perhaps human beings have always lived in exciting times. We certainly do. Everything is alive with activity and, though sometimes we don't quite know where the world is going, it appears to be busily on its way. Every corner of life is in bud and much of it is in flower; where we see no improvement, we note at least struggle. The striving of others engages us long after the days of our great exertions are over. We place ourselves in the position of those still in the contest and lovingly rehearse their every move in our minds.

If Janet had cared about the fortunes of her city or the fate of the wretched of the earth, or if she had focused her attention on the progress of medicine or even on developments in a favorite sport, she may never have felt that she had had enough. The movement of things fascinates us. We can sit in front of the fire, never tiring of the dancing flames. Many find the fiftieth season of baseball they watch as full of magic as the first. The trajectory of balls, planes drawing vapor trails in the sky, soaring birds, circus tumblers, cars hurtling at high speeds, and people waving their arms in the distance capture our attention and yield delight.

Above all else, we love the movement of human lives. We want to hear stories about what happens to people and what they do, about their backgrounds, their exploits, and their fates. We have an insatiable appetite for gossip about famous individuals and a fascination with the greats of history. People spend an astonishing amount of time speculating about who loves whom, and who believes what and why. We want to know what people value and about the lives such commitments create.

When we don't know the stories of people, we make them up. An old woman I once knew, shut in for a winter too cold for her to brave, sat like a cat at the window of her apartment all day, watching the activities on the street. She noted people coming home for lunch, strangers driving to her neighbors' doors, husbands and wives going off together and returning alone. She concocted stories out of these intriguing events. The exercise of her sense of drama so enriched her life that winter became her favorite time of year. Her seat by the window gave her a full view of fictive virtue and folly.

The question, therefore, is not how we can get interested in all that goes on in the world, but how we can fail to care. Everyone we meet has a story worth relating and experiences to offer that will instruct or amuse. The faces of people and the words we overhear, the bug that walks across the kitchen floor, the latest event reported in the news all grab our minds and take them on a journey. Wonder, Aristotle said, is the beginning of philosophy, but it is also the perpetual spur to construct an exciting and satisfying life.

Here, as elsewhere, the key is to expand our ego-boundaries to encompass neighbors, the community, if possible the entire human race. Such growth of self enables us to participate in the joy and energy of countless others. To say that we have seen it all is laughable. No one has seen next spring, and no one knows what inventions will make life better and what splendid music will make it sweeter soon. The papers are full of obituaries for the famous people who have died, but they never record the birth of persons who will make important contributions and become eminent decades from now. All of that is in the womb of the future, and to see what that greatest of mothers produces is one of the lasting pleasures of life.

Tiredness with Life

All it takes to overcome tiredness with life is to open our eyes. The world is throbbing with energy and promise, and if we can view it as kin to us, as our home, as in some sense ours, its movement will forever hold our gaze. The fascination abides even if we are too weak to do much more than see what happens next. We need simply to immerse ourselves in the energy of life all around us, as fish do swimming in the throbbing sea.

7

Death and the Rebirth of Energy

Death All Around

From time to time, life the terrorist takes one or two of us out to shoot. As in a violent dictatorship, there is no explanation why *these* among us, and why *now*. Friends and enemies, the young and the old, the healthy and the sick drop away. They disappear into nothingness and our memory of them fades as we wait for our turn to be forgotten.

Some of our children's friends died while in high school. Everyone knows people struck down in the prime of life by mindless accident or heart attack or cancer. But the sky permanently darkens for the old; they live under siege, encircled by death. When her close friends died, my mother reached out to renew relations with people whom she had not seen in years. As *they* passed on, she expanded the circle further by tracking down lost childhood acquaintances to share memories. Before long, all but two or three of the people she had known were gone, and she was left living in a world populated mainly by the dead.

It may seem easy to explain dying if we can connect it to something we have done. Helping to fight an outbreak of ebola or even smoking three packs a day makes it unsurprising that one dies. Yet even there a mystery persists: inexplicably, others more reckless survive. And often, ambushed by misfortune, it is the innocent who die. I remember a young woman, resplendent in pregnancy, pinned against a mailbox by a runaway car. Neither she nor her unborn child could suspect that a midday walk would turn into their Golgotha.

The thought that death is inevitable can paralyze a person. When it first occurs, usually in the early teens, we contemplate a time when we will no longer be, and the world without us presents a dreadful prospect. The later recognition that such a world will not be badly off, that in fact it will not even miss us, is even more horrible. But it is true, suggesting that we cannot reconcile ourselves to death without accepting our insignificance. This difficult task requires dealing with the baffling contradiction between the centrality of each private self to itself and the cosmic unimportance of them all.

Some think that fearing death is really dread of the process of dying or of what lies beyond. But the idea that we will not be able to continue with our projects is far more frightening than either of these concerns. That the time will come when we can no longer hug our loved ones or swim in the sea, that in just a few years we will not be able to run or speak or hear the song of birds, freezes the joints and the heart. A sense of personal loss cascades down on us until we feel we are drowning in sorrow.

The deepest revulsion to being no more comes, then, from the alarming thought that someday we will not be able to do the things we like. Fear of death, therefore, is simply our love of life served with summons and deadline. The momentum of our activities and the energy burning in us rebel at the thought of this limit; how could there be an end to something so joyous and so fine? Since life is devoted only to itself, the task of making our energy accept, even affirm, its own cessation is daunting and contradictory.

Our thoughts and our feelings are also contradictory. We *know* that everyone dies, and we can step back and think that a hundred years from now none of us will be alive. We can repeat with conviction what an old friend of mine, now dead, used to say: "You only live once, but if you play your cards right, that should be enough." Yet when emotions convert such abstract thoughts into vivid reality, our skin crawls. We cannot *feel* our way into the threatening inevitable: feeling that we will die is to feel dead already.

The sense that we have only so many more days, even though we don't know how many, is particularly worrying. Next year at this time I may be gone, one says to oneself, and if not next year then shortly thereafter. Our weakness combined with the uncertainties of the world creates the impression that we grope our way along the dark tunnel that is life. The ground might drop away at any moment: I might die in my sleep tonight or in a car wreck in the morning.

This line of thought leads directly into the chamber of skeletons. Soon we live not only with our own death but with the passing of everyone we know, of generation after generation, of the human race, of all living creatures, of the universe. We see crippled old people when our children play and every smiling face reveals a shriveled skull. When we behold only death, life loses its point; all human effort seems futile, all human hope misplaced. We move among the dead and fail to note that we are moving, that we live.

The Sun (and Life) Peek Through

Fixation on death makes us forget about everything wonderful in life. Dwelling on the horror of the no more causes us to overlook the beauty even of death when it slips in painlessly and in season. Ceaseless attention to the dark blinds us to the fact that we live in the sun, that challenges are exhilarating and our activities satisfy. In truth, the grim forecast that we'll die is, through most of life, irrelevant. Of course we die. But why should that spoil breakfast?

Waiting for death is a losing proposition: those who expect to die are disappointed day after day and, when their expectation is at last fulfilled, they are not likely to have a chance to enjoy it. Level-headed people get on with their lives, recognizing that a distant event cannot take anything away from what is good. That a fine meal will reappear in much altered form tomorrow does not make eating futile or unenjoyable. That sunsets last minutes and not weeks leaves their beauty untouched. And nothing would be gained, and much lost, if conversations or orgasms were sustained for years.

If anything, sunsets and orgasms mean more precisely because, like life, they are passing moments of joy. We love variety and structure and bite-size realities: nothing is special without context and limit. Watching the sun set over the sea is a fitting culmination to the day; but watched too long, sunsets lose their charm and intrude on the activities of the evening. *When* and *for how long* are central questions about everything we do. We live best when we find a suitable time for each activity and quit it before it is too late.

Letting go is a difficult skill to master. We need it daily to delegate responsibility, to move on to the next challenge, to allow others to make their own mistakes, and to let our children grow into adults. Yet our culture teaches that we can have it all, that we must control things and should never hang it up. The desire for the infinite and the inability to say "Enough!" torture our souls. Like Faust, the mythical devourer of experiences, we refuse to be satisfied. We want everything forever: success, money, admiration, and unwavering love. We want life everlasting.

Perhaps we could learn from our children. They spend the day at the beach building things that will not survive the next tide. They enjoy the process, give themselves to their activity with total devotion, take pride in what they built, and then leave it all without regrets. Adults, by contrast, want everything saved, everything to last. We seem to forget that playing for keeps is not *playing* at all.

Humans were not made for infinity. Too much of anything tires us or wears us out. Even when we don't admit it, our souls cry out to leave well enough alone. For most of us, control over a vast sum of money would create bafflement. Love for too many always forces painful choices. When institutions get too large, they lose their homey feel, and big government is rightly charged with inhumanity.

We live best in a world of finite, rounded, and comfortable shapes. As with the fairy tales of our childhood, we

Death and the Rebirth of Energy

love predictable beginnings and satisfying ends. Even the Arabian stories of the *Thousand and One Nights* had to stop for the listener to enjoy a cozy sense of completion. Shapeless stretches of space and unfinished time make a featureless desert of the mind.

The need for structure is wisely acknowledged by religious accounts of the history of the world. In the Judeo-Christian tradition, the course of events from creation to last judgment constitutes a satisfying and complete story, with heaven and hell serving only as afterthoughts. Human life replays this drama: all the action occurs between birth and death and makes, when things work right, a meaningful and integrated whole.

We stress the unified pattern of life by solemnizing its terminal points and its great events. Birth and death become, in this way, sacred occasions, as do marriage and reaching puberty. Celebrating these moments of existence and relating them to each other turn what might otherwise seem a disconnected series of events into organized and significant lives. This makes it possible for us to think that we have run our course, that we have done what could be expected and can now rest.

The notion of life as a completable pattern of development or sequence of activities has undergone expansion in the last few centuries. We no longer think of the natural lifespan as thirty or forty or even fifty years. As a result, people today do a lot more before they die than prior generations. But whether human life lasts fifty or a hundred years, it still has structure and limits. No matter how long we stay vigorous, we have not drunk of the fountain of everlasting youth. The pattern remains: no one escapes the pains of growing up, and the only way to elude old age is to die young.

Seasons

A classmate in my first year of college had great difficulty focusing on his work. He failed, took a year off and then tried his hand at studying again. The second failure fixated him on getting an undergraduate degree; he spent nearly twenty years in halting efforts before he gave up. The lost decades put him in a time warp and ruined his life.

At nearly forty, he was still taking notes in class and trying to date young coeds. Everything he attempted was out of synch or out of season. He embarked on a career at forty-five and thought about marriage past fifty. He tried to do what was appropriate to each age, but always too late. So he failed again and again, yet he could never get himself to write off the twenty years and start from where he was. Like a singer without a sense of timing, he lived his life two bars behind the band.

Those who live well know there is a rhythm to life; and in the music we make, timing is nearly all. Each stage of existence has activities suitable to it; at any other time, they simply don't work out. A day of carefree play in the sandbox is heaven at age three but a heartbreak if the person is thirty or eighty-three. Youthful sparring and boasting and pouting become insufferable when done by adults, and motherhood is a tragic imposition on a child.

The wisdom that there is a proper time for all things is convincingly expressed in *Ecclesiastes*. Contrary to the message of that book, however, when things are done in season, they are not "vanity and vexation of spirit" but the source of overwhelming joy. Food for hunger and sleep for weariness give comfort to the soul. Swinging one's racquet to connect with the ball at just the right angle at the perfect moment makes one's heart leap. And meeting a good person to love when circumstances and state of mind make one ready to settle down is as near heaven as a young person wants to be.

In some cases, later events undo earlier delights. Hasty love can land us in the doctor's office and uncontrolled desires may well lead to jail. But these are situations in which the pleasure contributes to the painful outcome or is bought directly at the price of it. Nothing like that obtains when natural developments invite us to act and to enjoy. Like running and laughter to a happy child, doing what we do well in the appropriate season is a costless benefit.

Whatever may happen next leaves such moments of grace untouched. We can, of course, grieve that the occasions do not endure, but when we do, we forget to see the rounded beauty of the season. Such events are not supposed to last; they cannot continue without losing their perfection. If we enjoy them for what they are, they leave nothing to be desired. We cannot improve the bold climb of a jet plane by slowing it down to last a day; as with all of life, it is better to let it fly.

A single action in the proper context can display such rightness or completeness no less than a way of living at a certain age. A person knocked at my door one day and said he was hungry. I didn't think of the danger of letting in a man I didn't know. I didn't tell myself that feeding the hungry was an obligation. I invited him to sit with me and eat. It was a moment of grace, the fitting response, something natural one human being does for another.

In Love with Life

My wife's father lived with such grace and dignity for months in the face of death. When he learned that his cancer was incurable, he took care of his affairs and arranged for his funeral. Then he went about his business without complaining, seeing the world work for a last, sweet time. Before he died, he went out West to see the wheatfields and the start of harvest.

All of us have done some complete and wonderful things here and there, and all of us know people who have lived in a way fitted to the season. Such actions or ways of being seem to come naturally to some, especially to children, though we admire them more when they are the result of thoughtful self-control or at least of sensible habits. To live an entire life in accordance with its seasons may be difficult, but there is no goal more worth pursuing.

To speak of our days on earth as consisting of seasons is to acknowledge that humans, like animals and plants, operate on a natural life cycle. This means that we must accomplish what we want within relatively few years. The people, like my dear friend from college, whose development is so slow that they appear to be on the five-hundred-year life plan, face unavoidable disaster. Those who think they can stay at the top of their form will suffer pain and disappointment.

The image of growth from bud to fruit is useful for depicting our development. We must be careful, however, not to think of life as paper-thin, aiming one-dimensionally at the production of some end. The fruits are many and, as any farmer knows, each stage in the unfolding of life has its beauty and integrity. From the light green of spring to the brown of the fall, every color of the forest holds a promise and tenders peace.

Death and the Rebirth of Energy

Once, some sunflower seeds fell from the birdfeeder outside our window, found a bit of soil, and germinated in the spring. I watched their growth each morning from the breakfast table with admiration for their work and wisdom. They struggled to capture the sun, stretching and gaining strength, and then burst into flower, adding magnificent suns to the one in the sky. The goldfinches could hardly wait for the seeds to fatten; they ate them, dropping a few on the ground. Long after the plants died, their proud remnants continued to stand as stiff, vertical perches for the birds.

Just like sunflowers, our lives can find meaning at each stage and not lose usefulness even after death. And if the glory of sunflowers can match the sun's, imagine the beauty of a well-formed human life! The complaint that we don't live forever is absurd if we consider what we can delight in and what we can accomplish while we do.

Luck and Work

Some people believe that viewing our condition by analogy with the life cycle of plants is or ought to be wrong. They think we are, as Santayana put it, too good for extinction and should, accordingly, live on without an end. To them, death is an indignity or a confession of failure whose hold over us we must deny or resist.

They are, of course, entirely right that we should not think we are like chipmunks and sunflowers unless we must. But is there an alternative? Even if we expect a richer life when we see God face to face, we still grow, flower, and decline in this one. Whatever may happen beyond, death still closes this life with a finality we cannot suspend. Facing the facts is no indignity; if we were dealt cards for poker, we cannot switch games to play chess.

Would it be better if we never died? That depends. Having to live thousands of years crippled, ill, or in physical agony is not a gift we want. If we never died, would we ever age? If we did not, we would miss too many of the wonderful stages in life, too much maturing and nearly all our hope. Could we even imagine what it would be like to have Adam, Alexander the Great, and Attila still walking around? Could the young ever think that a slot might open for them in the center, that it would ever be their turn?

Whoever takes it from the stage of inarticulate wish to well-formed thought realizes that the idea of endless life is a senseless dream. Death is not the enemy; it stings only when it comes out of season. So the most we can reasonably say is that, while things go well, we want an extra year or ten. This can be a sound goal, and good personal habits, sane social conditions, and improving medicine all contribute to its achievement. But it is only a goal, so there is no assurance that we will attain it.

Does this mean that in the end much or everything about life is a matter of luck? Some people think of what we do as the outcome of how our circumstances shape us, and of our circumstances as the result of accident. This means that we can't take much credit for what was done and can't hold much hope for molding what will come. The way to understand the human condition, they say, is to see how things fall out; the key is to attend to what happens and not to what we do.

Like most extreme views, this belief holds a grain of truth. A great deal about life is a matter of luck. That we were born healthy and didn't die young, that our parents loved instead of starving or molesting us, and that we continue to enjoy the benefits of drive and brains rather than facing life as lazy, deformed imbeciles are all largely past our power to affect. With respect to the seasons of life, in particular, fortune must favor us to survive the first. As Aristotle knew, though perhaps no better than we do, one cannot say that those who die young lived a full life or lived well.

Yet one can easily overestimate the power of fate. All around us, we can see good fortune squandered and disaster reversed. The contribution we make to our future is undeniable: try not chewing and swallowing for a week even though the refrigerator is full. Talents don't turn into achievements without effort, and sustained trying is something we do rather than something that happens to us.

The actions we take and what we fail to attempt exercise a profound influence on our lives. Sometimes we get lucky and unexpected opportunities present themselves; but they remain worthless unless we seize them. At the other extreme, those in the depths of despair can sometimes bounce off the bottom by continuing to fight or work. Energy and ideas tend to bring results: although people who never give up don't always succeed, those who don't try are simply washed away.

The most productive attitude to aging and death, therefore, is not to lament our misfortune but to make the remainder of life as good as it can be. Interestingly, that is the natural response of persons struggling to deal with tragedy. Older people who go blind or lose their partners soon manage to find comfort even in their constricted lives. For many struck by misfortune, much-appreciated small satisfactions take the place of grand projects. Even young quadriplegics begin to see new meaning in life about a year after their paralyzing accident.

This gift of nature can sometimes be hastened by deliberate effort. Making the necessary changes in our expectations and enjoying the activities still open to us can help us adjust to narrowing horizons. And viewing death as an unavoidable natural event robs it of much of its horror. These are adjustments we can make to increase the level of our comfort with declining life. The range of our control over events is not, in the end, what matters. What really counts is that the world created by what we do and what befalls us have the cozy feel of home.

Old Age

My mother once said that old age is not for the faint of heart. At best, it is a vulnerable time without heartening prospects. Like those who sit in a restaurant late at night or stay in the theater past the last performance, we witness the dismantling of the scene. The chairs and tables are put away, light after light is turned out, soon there is dark. Even if we have no apprehension about the future, we feel a sense of sadness and of loss.

Things get much worse if recurrent pain or chronic disease attack. For many people, old age is sequential organ failure. For others, defect in a single organ is enough to render life a difficult struggle. For everyone, aging is the death of possibilities, a steady reduction of what we can do and how well we can do it. From the earliest signs of decline to the time when the hands won't stop shaking, the process cannot be reversed; one by one, we give up the skills we worked so hard to attain.

Aggressive public health measures and wonderful improvements in medicine have made life longer and better for many people. But longer life means an increasing number of the sick and weak in slow decline. This is a problem unique to the modern world, and the cost of caring for everyone who suffers from the illnesses and disabilities of old age threatens to be a grave political issue for generations. More important from a personal standpoint, each of us faces the likelihood of spending many years on the downslope of life.

This naturally leads people to ask what they can do to make aging bearable. But this is the wrong question, aiming for too little in the last years of our love affair with life. The right question is how we can make aging a glorious and fitting end to an exceptional journey. That this is possible at all may come as a surprise to people who spend their energy lamenting wrinkles and graying hair. Yet it clearly is, and those who age with grace seem to have an answer worth exploring.

Old age offers benefits no other time of life provides. The stilling of drives yields a peace we have never known before. If we permit this calm to settle on the world the way motionless moonlight sits on the bushes in the yard, everything acquires beauty and unspeakable meaning. We come to feel distanced from action and from the partiality that goes with it. We learn to see the world as one views ancient history.

When action is called for, we must of course still be able to give an account of ourselves. But now knowledge frames activity as part of a luminous world; we have seen these things before, we know where they lead, we know how people feel about them. This is not the peace that passes all understanding, but the repose that occurs because of it. We nod our heads comprehending and even affirming what goes on, without the desire to possess or to control.

Learning to let go comes, in this way, to occupy center stage in the later years. Not surprisingly, some older persons tend to compensate for slippage of mastery over their surroundings by aggressively reasserting control. This often takes the form of giving others precise instructions about what to do and then criticizing their performance. Next to incessant complaining, this is the activity most objectionable to those who care for the old, and the point of greatest conflict.

Though this is a hard lesson, we need to learn that some things simply don't matter. Having the dishes stacked just right, the towels smoothed down in their proper place and the curtains pulled to exactly one inch of maximum opening are not matters of cosmic significance. If we can't fix them that way ourselves, it may be best to leave them alone. The moment we look the other way, the annoyance disappears. We can shrug our shoulders and start enjoying new configurations of the world around us.

Laughter is always the ultimate weapon, and it works best when we direct it at our own debility. "Look at the things I can't do," a ninety-three-year-old woman once told me, chuckling. The twinkle in her eyes was clear evidence that she had made her peace. The comment was not complaint but curiosity. Why should it not be natural that at eighty we can't play tennis any more and at ninety we can't thread a needle? She knew that there is always *something* we can do, and doing it brings enjoyment.

Death and the Rebirth of Energy

Retaining the purposes of earlier years, on the other hand, causes unending pain. Another old person told me that he continued wanting to do the things he had always done, but his hands and arms and legs were no longer able. In his own eyes he was still forty or fifty years old, and he had great difficulty accepting the physical limits on his insatiable will. The strategy of wanting to do a little more than we easily can stretches us and may bring achievement. But wanting a great deal more leads only to disappointment and collapse.

Activities out of season are saddest when they represent major, continuing commitments. Unable to put up with seeing an aging face across the breakfast table, some people divorce and marry persons younger than their children. No way of fleeing old age works; this one often has the special disadvantage of achieving the opposite of what we hope. After the initial charm of the relation wears off (or before), the difference in years brings one's own age into exaggerated focus. Soon, married bliss gives way to resentment and jealousy.

The best thing to do with old age is to accept it and to enjoy the glorious glimpses of life it presents. Up to a point at least, the mind rises to the mountains as the body goes down. The survey of existence this offers is beyond compare. We can continue to enjoy some activities, and we can enjoy the control over ourselves that makes us live happily in a smaller world. In one respect, the world need not be smaller: we can take an interest in how well others do. Their energy always surrounds us, and we can love our past in loving them. We can also be loved, perhaps by humans and certainly by pets, to make the last years meaningful and rich.

In Love with Life

Death and Renewal

A distinguished surgeon once announced that there is no good death and no dignified passing. I understand the doctor's burning desire to resist what he perceived as the ultimate evil. Still, he was wrong. There is a good death and it comes when our energy runs out. Such a death is appropriate because, without drive and intensity, there is nothing more to do. And we resist it no more: we are spent and the physical quiet invites eternal peace.

We see such deaths among the very old and the very sick. Understandably, they think that further life under their circumstances is a pointless torture and that death is a blessing. Suicide and euthanasia acquire significance in this context: continued physical existence is of no benefit to an individual in intractable pain or to people who are done with life. No serious religious person and no one who loves life can maintain that the continued travail of our biological organism is worth its cost in human suffering. The body, after all, is not the human being; we love and celebrate its intelligent motion, not its cells and chemicals.

If things fall out right, we can die a good death to cap off a good life. But we may face the sadness of our turn coming before the energy runs out. Life is too good to give up without a fight. Rabbits caught in the clutches of the fox struggle for awhile, and a few get away. But when it becomes hopeless they go limp, resigning themselves to their fate. This is nature's strategy, and we know no better. We must fight until near death but, in the end, surrender ourselves in a moment of grace. If nothing else, we can cheat death by going in peace.

Death and the Rebirth of Energy

When the time comes, we must surround ourselves with life. In a bustling hospital or in a loving home, let everyone get on with their activities. To die in the midst of energy is not to die at all, but to transfer one's life and hopes to those who carry on. The continuity of our lives and our personalities makes the death of any one individual an event of little moment: the great celebration of existence goes on.

On the personal side, anyone can be cheerful by forgetting about death or depressed by thinking about it all the time. Mastery of life is to remember death and yet live joyously.

The time will doubtless come for each of us, if not for the universe at large, to cease from care; but our passage through life will have added a marvelous episode to the tale of things.

GEORGE SANTAYANA,
Realms of Being

Photo by Billy Kingsley, Vanderbilt University

Few professional philosophers enjoy a greater reputation, respect, and admiration than John Lachs. One of the leading interpreters of the American philosophical tradition, Lachs is Centennial Professor of Philosophy at Vanderbilt University. His previous books include *Intermediate Man* (1981), *Mind and Philosophers* (1987), and *The Relevance of Philosophy to Life* (1995).

IN LOVE WITH LIFE

was composed electronically using
Adobe Garamond types, with displays in Diotima and Type
Embellishments Two.
The book was printed on 60# Glatfelter Supple Opaque paper
and Smyth sewn and cased in Arrestox B linen
by Thomson-Shore, Inc.
The dust jacket was printed in four colors by
Vanderbilt University Printing Services.
Book and dust jacket designs are the work of Gary Gore.
Published by Vanderbilt University Press
Nashville, Tennessee 37235